50 GREAT AMERICAN PLACES

ESSENTIAL HISTORIC SITES ACROSS THE U.S.

BRENT D. GLASS

FOREWORD BY DAVID MCCULLOUGH

SIMON & SCHUSTER PAPERBACKS

NEW YORK   LONDON   TORONTO   SYDNEY   NEW DELHI

Simon & Schuster Paperbacks
An Imprint of Simon & Schuster, Inc.
1230 Avenue of the Americas
New York, NY 10020

First Simon & Schuster trade paperback edition March 2016

SIMON & SCHUSTER PAPERBACKS and colophon are
registered trademarks of Simon & Schuster, Inc.

For information about special discounts for bulk purchases,
please contact Simon & Schuster Special Sales at 1-866-506-1949
or business@simonandschuster.com.

The Simon & Schuster Speakers Bureau can bring authors to your
live event. For more information or to book an event, contact the
Simon & Schuster Speakers Bureau at 1-866-248-3049
or visit our website at www.simonspeakers.com.

Interior design by Ruth Lee-Mui

Manufactured in the United States of America

10   9   8   7   6   5   4   3

Library of Congress Cataloging-in-Publication Data

Glass, Brent D., author.
   50 great American places : essential historic sites across the U.S. / Brent D. Glass ;
foreword by David McCullough.
      pages   cm
   1. Historic sites—United States—Guidebooks. I. Title. II. Title: Fifty great American
places.
 E159.G539 2016
 973—dc23 2015031714

ISBN 978-1-4516-8203-8
ISBN 978-1-4516-8204-5 (ebook)

To the memory of my parents,

JOSEPH AND CORINNE GLASS,

who inspired my love of history and learning

CONTENTS

PLACES BY STATE

Author's note: Some essays in this book describe more than one place; therefore, the total number of sites is greater than fifty. But most readers will agree that the United States has many more than fifty great places. I hope you will add to the list.

The list of places by state includes the town or city in which the site is located or, in some cases, the nearest town to that site. The site mentioned on this list is the major subject of each essay.

ALABAMA
Huntsville/Saturn V Rocket

ARIZONA
Tucson/Mission San Xavier del Bac

ARKANSAS
Little Rock/Little Rock Central High School

CALIFORNIA
Burbank/Warner Bros. Studio
La Jolla/Salk Institute

SOUTH DAKOTA
Pine Ridge/Wounded Knee Monument

TENNESSEE
Nashville/Ryman Auditorium

TEXAS
San Antonio/The Alamo

UTAH
Salt Lake City/Temple Square

VIRGINIA
Charlottesville/Monticello
Yorktown/Virginia Peninsula

WASHINGTON
Richland/Hanford B Reactor

WASHINGTON, D.C.
The National Mall

WISCONSIN
Spring Green/Taliesin

WYOMING
Yellowstone National Park

FOREWORD

BY DAVID MCCULLOUGH

When Brent Glass, a friend of many years, first told me about the book he planned to write, I said immediately I thought it a marvelous idea and that it would fill a real need. I also wondered to myself why in the world I hadn't thought of it. Journeys to great historic sites had been high points for me since boyhood and have remained a mainstay of my work from the time I embarked on my first book. But no, I thought. With all his scholarship and professional experience as a public historian, Brent was just the one for the task. Indeed, I know of no one who knows more about American historic sites. Public historians believe that history should be accessible to all, that it is much too important to leave to academics alone or solely to the classroom, and as a public historian Brent is a national leader.

We first met in 1989, at the Centennial of the Johnstown Flood, and were happy to discover how many interests we had in common. He was then head of the Pennsylvania Historical and Museum Commission. Later, during the years he served as director of the National Museum of American History at the Smithsonian, our paths crossed more and more, and our ensuing friendship became one of the prime rewards of our shared interest in how much of the story of our country is to be found all around us, as part of the immense American landscape.

As it was for Brent, my first journey into history began at about age ten with a visit with my parents to a historical landmark, Fort Necessity in western Pennsylvania, some sixty miles southeast of our home in Pittsburgh. The site of the first skirmish of the French and Indian War, it is where young Lieutenant Colonel George Washington and his troops suffered a humiliating defeat. There was not a whole lot to be seen—a replica of a small wooden fort set in an open field—but it certainly made a lasting impression.

In grade school we learned more of what had happened right in Pittsburgh during the eighteenth century and that Brent gives appropriate attention to in his chapter on the Forks of the Ohio. Later, while in high school, I had the good fortune to travel further into history during a spring vacation road trip with a friend and his parents through much of Virginia, with stops at Monticello and Mount Vernon, and the experience opened my mind and imagination to history as nothing yet had.

Over the years since, my wife, Rosalee, and I made a point of taking our own children to historic sites across much of the country whenever possible, and always with pronounced results. One of our sons tells me he still remembers the family expedition to the Custer Battlefield (now called Little Bighorn Battlefield) in Montana in every detail, while his brother loves to recount going to Mystic Seaport on the coast of Connecticut on a cold, nasty day to go on board the famous whaling ship *The Morgan* and listen to the tour guide tell all about the ship and its voyages. To this day, he says, he can't drive by Mystic without feeling the pull of those stories.

And the effect can carry down the line. Our youngest daughter's reaction to the Frontier Culture Museum in the Shenandoah Valley, in Staunton, Virginia, a beautiful complex of early farms of different varieties, was everything a parent could hope for. Twenty years later she would see the same response in her seven-year-old son.

But until now there has never been a guidebook like this by someone with such a background as Brent Glass. He has not only traveled to each of the fifty historic sites he describes, but to another hundred or more besides. In lectures he likes to stress "the power of place," and certainly there is that aplenty in the panorama of places to be found in these pages.

The geographic reach of the book extends north, south, coast to coast, and beyond to Pearl Harbor. At the same time, as he points out, a chronological span of nearly a thousand years is to be found in the ancient Cahokia Mounds in western Illinois and the great Gateway Arch in St. Louis built in the 1960s, both on the Mississippi River and only eight miles apart. Even greater is the reach into the past of the prehistoric site called Meadowcroft, again near Pittsburgh, where human habitation dates back 16,000 years.

Clearly, too—and admirably—the choice of subjects here leaves no doubt that history, so often dominated by politics and war, comprises far more. And so here, also, one will find ample reminders of who we are as a people, and why we are the way we are, as expressed in American art, music, science and technology, medicine, manufacturing, and literature.

I was delighted to find included Red Cloud, Nebraska, the childhood home of the great American novelist Willa Cather. As Brent writes, no one explored the theme of the American pioneers and their impact on the land more eloquently than she. The town of Red Cloud, so much of which has been preserved, is, as he says, "a living monument," and beyond the town, out on the prairie, a white-frame farmhouse, the home of one Annie Pavelka, has also been preserved. As history customarily evaluates those from our past, Annie Pavelka was nobody, no more than any of the thousands of other pioneer women who persevered through tremendous adversity. But Annie Pavelka and her story were the inspiration for Willa Cather's famous masterpiece *My Ántonia,* and to stand there beside the storm cellar into which she rushed her children when tornadoes struck is to feel "the power of place" in no uncertain terms.

How fitting that such architectural and engineering triumphs as Grand Central Terminal, the Brooklyn Bridge, and the Gateway Arch figure prominently here. Among those sites to which I have never been as yet, I'm now drawn especially to Edison's Laboratory in New Jersey and the Salk Institute in California, a tribute to Dr. Jonas Salk and architect Louis Kahn, two of the great geniuses of the twentieth century.

Paging through the book again on a second reading, I can't help but think of how difficult it must have been deciding what to leave out. After all, fifty selections hardly begins to represent the full number and variety of places with much to tell us. There is Carpenters' Hall in Philadelphia, a Georgian gem of a building and the place where the first Continental Congress met in 1774. What a wonder that something so immense all began in a setting so small! But the same may be said for the Dayton, Ohio, home and bicycle shop of the Wright brothers, both of which have been preserved intact, just as they were, at the Ford Museum in Dearborn, Michigan. No matter how many times I have stood in that crowded little bicycle shop, I still feel overwhelming amazement that an idea that would so change the world took shape there of all places.

The many hours I have spent at the Adams house in Quincy, Massachusetts, and the Truman house in Independence, Missouri, were for me as important as any part of the research that went into understanding both men. And one needs time in such settings not only to observe closely but to think about what one sees.

There is a bedroom door on the second floor of the Adams house, for example, on the other side of which Nabby Adams, the daughter of John and Abigail, was subjected to a mastectomy without anesthetics while her father and mother stood waiting in the hall, suffering intense agony of another kind. He felt, Adams wrote, as though he were living in the book of Job.

Then there is the old linoleum kitchen floor in the Truman house, in the middle of which runs a substantial crack. Rather than addressing the problem with a costly new linoleum floor, the Trumans had the crack neatly tacked in place, and so it remains, perfect evidence of plain, old-fashioned, midwestern common sense and economy still on display.

For all my books I have made a point of going where the story took place wherever that might be—to see for myself, to soak it up, to smell the air, to note the slant of a morning beam of light through a window, to listen to the sounds of the night, and to walk the walk as those others did. It is essential. And, yes, it is part of the joy of learning. But then, one need not be writing a book to find the benefits and joy that can come from time spent at historic sites, and here in the pages of this fine book by Brent Glass one will find reason in abundance to get out on the road to see for yourself what you haven't yet seen or retrace favorite previous steps a second time.

INTRODUCTION

Celebrating the anniversary of American independence on a high mesa in the Rocky Mountains is quite a contrast with past years, when I hosted friends each Fourth of July on the rooftop of the Smithsonian's National Museum of American History. Instead of watching fireworks bursting over the National Mall and the Potomac River, this year I witnessed a stunning show of lightning over the Colorado Plateau. The stars in the western sky outnumbered the Roman candles going off in distant mountain towns. Three wild horses strolled by, surprisingly close in the shadows. After a day visiting the rocky remains of homes abandoned by the Ancestral Puebloan people eight hundred years ago, I reflected on the distance I have traveled in time and space to essential historic sites across the United States.

This book tells the story of America through places that matter in our history. These great American places represent fundamental themes in our national narrative: the compelling story of democracy and self-government, the dramatic impact of military conflict, the powerful role of innovation and enterprise, the inspiring achievements of diverse cultural traditions, and the defining influence of the land and its resources.

The connections between places, people, and events reveal a national narrative that is often surprising, sometimes tragic, and always engaging.

These themes and places intersect in significant ways. The struggle to create and sustain democracy is evident from the National Mall in Washington, D.C., to Seneca Falls, New York, from Hudson, Ohio, to Little Rock, Arkansas. Military conflicts at sites from Yorktown to Fort Sumter, from Little Bighorn to Pearl Harbor have changed our history. Historic places from Slater Mill to Edison's Laboratory, from Ford River Rouge to Silicon Valley reveal the transformative impact of innovation and enterprise. America's cultural diversity is expressed in Emma Lazarus's poem on the Statue of Liberty extending "world-wide welcome" to immigrants, in Ryman Auditorium in Nashville and Preservation Hall in New Orleans, and at architectural landmarks from the Palace of the Governors to Monticello to Taliesin. America's response to the land and its resources is found from the Hoover Dam to Yellowstone National Park, and from the utopian communities of New Harmony, Indiana, to the beauty of California's Golden Gate. There are sites, too, that remind us of heartbreaking chapters of our past, from Salem, Massachusetts, to Minidoka, Idaho.

In addition to using a thematic framework to shape the selection of historic sites, I also included places to ensure a wide range of locations and time periods. The book begins with the National Mall followed by a number of great American places in chronological order according to when each site achieved its greatest significance. The list is not arranged, as someone once asked me, in order of importance. Every one of these sites is important because they all illustrate that history is not inevitable. People make history through the choices and decisions that define their time. Americans chose to declare independence from England, write great novels about slavery and race, invent a machine that flies, and build and use the atomic bomb.

My own journey through American history began with a road trip when I was ten. My parents packed my brother, Keith, sister, Jodi, and me into our old Hudson; drove to Washington; and introduced us to the museums and monuments along the National Mall and beyond. That experience sparked my love of history. I was fortunate to attend graduate school in the 1970s, at a time when the field of public history emerged into greater prominence. The purpose and value of communicating about the past—not only in classrooms and scholarly publications but also in public forums—became increasingly accepted. I recognized the importance of making history accessible to all.

As a public historian, I am committed to engaging and informing anyone who is curious about our history. Throughout my career, I have worked to translate academic language into public language, from field-work in North Carolina to leading Pennsylvania's public history organization to directing the Smithsonian's National Museum of American History. I continue to enjoy the privilege of working alongside colleagues who share my commitment to public history and the passion for preserving our collective public memory—the sites, buildings, artifacts, collections, documents, and oral histories that form our national identity. Without the work of colleagues at the great historic places in this country and the pioneering efforts of the preservationists who preceded us, we would lose an understanding of who we are as a nation.

I envision *50 Great American Places* as a contribution to historical literacy. Historical literacy is more than simply knowing the names of leaders or when famous battles were fought. It involves understanding the context of historical events and how events are connected. Above all, history is a resource for understanding our own lives and times. Sustaining a democratic society in America is not possible without citizens who know and love its history. We cannot participate fully in democracy without historical knowledge.

Finally, this book is a guide for people who, like my family more than fifty years ago, decide to make their own journey to America's historic places. Authenticity—sights, sounds, smells, the transcendent experience of standing where Lincoln stood, seeing what Georgia O'Keeffe saw—cannot be experienced vicariously through photographs in a book or digital images on a website. Some of the great American places described in this book are well known, such as Gettysburg Battlefield or Monticello. Others are remote: it may take a long time to travel to Wounded Knee or Hanford or Red Cloud. But the journey to these locations plays a large part in understanding their significance—the tragedy of the Indian Wars, the consequences of the Manhattan Project, the achievements of American artists, writers, and architects. Seeing the real thing stirs our imagination and inspires us to pursue greater knowledge about our shared heritage.

—Mesa Verde, Colorado
July 4, 2014

AUTHOR'S NOTE

There is a website for every one of the 50 Great American Places in this book. Each is listed at the end of its related essay along with websites for places or collections that are thematically connected to the subject. In addition, I have included websites for Nearby Places that may be of interest to the history traveler.

The National Park Service (NPS) websites are uniformly reliable and good resources for information about national parks, battlefields, historic sites, memorials, and monuments. The NPS sites also include good maps and updated information about programs and events. Websites generally provide current information about hours of operation, fees, and construction that might limit access to certain sites or collections.

1

THE NATIONAL MALL

WASHINGTON, D.C.

The National Mall

Democracy is the great achievement of America. It is more than our form of government; it is synonymous with our national identity and our national character. Although we associate democracy with ideas like freedom and equality, there is one physical place in America where our values, ideals, and traditions are celebrated every day for the world to see—the National Mall in Washington, D.C.

A visitor can stand at the Washington Monument at the center of the National Mall and see almost all the major landmarks of this remarkable public space that spans more than three hundred acres and stretches out over two miles. To the east, there is the gleaming dome of the Capitol and the superb museums of the Smithsonian Institution. The National Gallery of Art and the United States Botanic Garden, with their unsurpassed collections of art and horticulture, also occupy prominent sites. Within a short walk, there is a stunning variety of architectural styles from the Smithsonian Castle by James Renwick Jr. to the National Gallery's East Building by I. M. Pei.

The western half of the Mall includes a memorial landscape that honors the great leaders of our nation—George Washington, Thomas Jefferson, Abraham Lincoln, Franklin Delano Roosevelt, and Dr. Martin Luther King Jr.—as well as the men and women who have served in the major wars of our history. These monuments and memorials not only honor the people who have shaped our history but also reflect the creativity of artists, architects, and sculptors. From the classical designs of Henry Bacon (Lincoln Memorial) and John Russell Pope (Jefferson Memorial) to the powerfully abstract form of Maya Lin's Vietnam Veterans Memorial and the historical symbolism of the National Museum of African American History and Culture designed by Freelon Adjaye Bond/SmithGroup, the Mall offers visitors a three-dimensional lesson in architectural history. Farther west across the Potomac are Arlington National Cemetery and George Washington's home, Mount Vernon.

The design of the Mall itself represents a major chapter in the history of urban planning in America. Although Pierre L'Enfant's original plan for Washington included a broad open area from the Capitol to the Potomac River, the area we call the National Mall evolved slowly through the nineteenth century when the major projects included the Capitol, the first buildings of the Smithsonian, and Victorian-period landscaping. After the dedication of the Washington Monument (1888) Americans began to appreciate that the United States was emerging as a world power and that our national capital needed to reflect that power in its buildings, parks, and public places.

The single biggest influence on the design of the Mall was the 1902 plan of the Senate Park Commission, commonly known as the McMillan Commission for its chairman, Senator James McMillan of Michigan. The commission included leading architects and artists of the time— Daniel Burnham, Frederick Law Olmsted Jr., Charles F. McKim, and Augustus Saint-Gaudens. Their ideas have shaped the National Mall over the past century. Inspired by the World's Columbian Exposition held in Chicago in 1893, the McMillan Plan recommended a broad green park flanked by trees and classical buildings, adding new land to the west of the Washington Monument and locating the Lincoln Memorial at the Mall's western end. Although many elements of the Mall have changed in recent years, the central theme of a formal open space with open views from the Capitol to the Potomac and beyond has survived.

Since 1933, the National Park Service (NPS) has managed the National Mall, not an easy task given the need for a balance between public use, political initiatives, and preservation priorities. Every few years, proposals for new projects on the Mall generate passionate debate. Visitors to the enormously popular Vietnam Veterans Memorial (1982), for example, are surprised to learn that Maya Lin's design for this site was the subject of bitter criticism from some veterans' groups and architects who wanted a more traditional representation of soldiers in action. Advocates for historic preservation resisted the decision to locate the World War II Memorial at the heart of the west Mall out of concern that it would intrude on the view between the Washington Monument and the Lincoln Memorial. Years after the dedication of this memorial in 2004, spirited arguments persist on the merits of new memorials and whether to limit new construction on the Mall.

Do recent memorials and monuments on the National Mall achieve the timelessness and inspirational impact of their predecessors? Professor Michael J. Lewis of Williams College has written, "Monuments, because they are public art, must be legible. It is because of their ability to transcend time by connecting to primal human activities—passage, gathering, shelter—that the best monuments never look dated." On the National Mall, recent memorials to the Korean War, World War II, Franklin Delano Roosevelt, and Martin Luther King Jr. and the proposed memorial to Dwight D. Eisenhower resemble museum exhibitions that emphasize storytelling and entertaining rather than honoring and remembering. Furthermore, the proliferation of museums and the prospect of building more in the future—however worthy their mission—run the risk of fragmenting our understanding of American culture and history as well as reducing much-needed open space.

Although monuments, memorials, and museums serve as our public memory and patrimony, what truly animates the Mall and makes it such a central symbol of democracy are the ways people—famous and ordinary—have used it as a setting to make history. Marian Anderson's Easter Sunday concert in 1939, the anti–Vietnam War marches of the 1960s, and the NAMES Project Memorial Quilt in 1987 to commemorate lives lost in the AIDS epidemic took place here. The most famous demonstration was the August 28, 1963, March on Washington for Jobs and Freedom. With the Lincoln Memorial in the background, Dr. Martin Luther King Jr. addressed more than 250,000 people with his resounding "I Have a Dream" speech that defined the American civil rights movement.

With all this rich history, impressive architecture, and scenic beauty, the National Mall remains a place for people. Here, too, NPS faces the challenge of balancing physical maintenance and public access. Annual celebrations, such as the Cherry Blossom Festival and the Smithsonian Folk Festival, attract millions of people from all parts of the country and the world. Local residents enjoy playing softball and volleyball amid the formal public space. Throughout the year, people jog, bike, walk, and picnic. As NPS and preservationists determine the best long-term strategy, I hope that the Mall remains America's front porch—open, accessible, and free—a worthy wonder of a democratic society.

WEBSITES
The National Mall, www.nps.gov/mall
Smithsonian Institution, www.si.edu
National Gallery of Art, www.nga.gov

NEARBY PLACES
George Washington's Mount Vernon, www.mountvernon.org
Arlington National Cemetery, www.arlingtoncemetery.mil
United States Holocaust Memorial Museum, www.ushmm.org
Ford's Theatre National Historic Site, www.nps.gov/foth or
    www.fordstheatre.org
Frederick Douglass National Historic Site, www.nps.gov/frdo

2

THE MOUNDS AND THE ARCH

COLLINSVILLE, ILLINOIS/ST. LOUIS, MISSOURI

Cahokia Mounds

Nearly a thousand years separate the Cahokia Mounds in western Illinois from the Gateway Arch in St. Louis, Missouri. Yet the two sites, both powerful symbols of their respective civilizations, share prominent locations on opposite sides of the Mississippi River, less than eight miles apart. In the eleventh century, Cahokia was the largest city north of Mexico, a major center of what archaeologists call Mississippian culture. Between 1050 and 1200 its population soared to around 10,000, with as many as 30,000 inhabitants living in smaller villages within a fifty-mile radius. In 1250, Cahokia was larger than London! The most distinctive features of Cahokia were more than 120 earth-packed pyramids, or mounds, that served as centers of civic and religious life as well as elite residences. Without benefit of horses or wagons, the Cahokians built these mounds—platform, ridge-topped, and conical—at a prodigious rate.

At the state historic site near Collinsville, Illinois, visitors may climb Monks Mound, a great platform structure that stands ten stories high and covers more than 14 acres. A 5,000-square-foot wooden temple once stood on this mound, the home of the city's religious chief. West of Monks Mound is a reconstruction of Woodhenge, a circle of wooden posts 410 feet in diameter, used to mark seasonal change. To the south of the mound is the Grand Plaza, a tremendous engineering feat spanning more than 50 acres. The plaza was the setting for ceremonies and sporting events such as a popular game called "chunkey" in which two players scored points by throwing spears at a rolling stone. Archaeologists have found chunkey artifacts throughout the midwestern and southeastern United States and even eighteenth- and nineteenth-century travelers observed American Indians playing versions of the game.

Travelers' accounts and archaeological research have contributed knowledge of the extraordinary history and influence of the Cahokian culture. The first professional excavations were in the 1920s, followed by a WPA project in 1941, and generations of archaeologists have repeatedly revisited the site. They have made important discoveries about Cahokia's religious life, which centered on earth and sky gods and included human sacrifice. They have reconstructed the farming techniques of a corn-based agricultural society and documented an extensive commercial network. They discovered evidence of a wooden stockade that protected the city center from potential invaders.

Archaeologists have raised intriguing theories about why Cahokia expanded so suddenly around 1050. Some speculate that a supernova, a "guest star" four times brighter than Venus, appeared in the sky for nearly a month in July 1054, interpreted by Cahokians as a sign to launch a building boom; others believe a charismatic leader inspired the city's growth. They are less certain, however, about why residents began to leave the city and outer settlements in the late thirteenth century and disappeared completely by 1400.

Although it has been a World Heritage Site since 1982, Cahokia has always faced preservation challenges. Urban development in the St. Louis area routinely destroyed many mounds. Only the threat of highway construction in the 1960s and again in the twenty-first century generated funding for systematic investigations and created a sense of urgency to recover the trove of information still buried along the Mississippi. To protect the most important Cahokian sites, the state of Illinois purchased 2,200 acres and built an interpretive center, the starting point for walking tours (guided and self-guided) through the remains of the ancient settlement, offering tangible evidence that American Indians created a complex, prosperous, and densely populated city whose influence spread across the continent.

Just as Monks Mound dominated Cahokia in the eleventh century, the Gateway Arch rises above modern St. Louis as a symbol of its civic ambition and historical memory. It is the tallest man-made memorial in America and the largest steel memorial in the world. Designed by Eero Saarinen, a master of modernist architecture, and engineer Hannskarl Bandel, the arch is the centerpiece of a sixty-acre park created to revive the city's waterfront and commemorate its role in nineteenth-century westward expansion.

Saarinen designed an arch that is as tall as it is wide—630 feet. It consists of 142 steel sections supported by reinforced concrete and covered by a stainless steel skin. At its base, its legs are 54 feet wide

NATIONAL PARK SERVICE

Gateway Arch

and taper to a width of 17 feet at its peak. This narrowing effect and its triangular walls give the arch a graceful, soaring quality, yet it is designed to withstand earthquakes, lightning bolts, and the windstorms common in the region. A tram that runs through its center allows visitors to ride to the top for spectacular views as far as thirty miles—to Cahokia and beyond.

At the base of the arch is the Jefferson National Expansion Memorial with exhibits (now undergoing major renovation) on the Louisiana Purchase of 1803 and the Lewis and Clark expedition of 1804–1806, both pivotal moments in American history. For a bargain price of $15 million (about forty-two cents per acre in today's money), President Thomas Jefferson doubled the size of the United States. He commissioned two young officers—Meriwether Lewis and William Clark—to lead their Corps of Discovery on a journey from St. Louis to the Pacific Ocean, mapping the continent, collecting scientific information, and establishing peaceful relations with various American Indian nations.

The historical connection between St. Louis and the growth of America shaped the city's strategy to secure support for its civic and economic agenda. This approach was effective in 1904 to attract both the Summer Olympics and the Louisiana Purchase Exposition, a world's fair that attracted twenty million visitors. In the 1930s, city leaders again tapped into the legacy of Jefferson and westward expansion to earn approval from the Roosevelt administration for riverfront revitalization that included plans for a major memorial. When it opened in 1967, the Gateway Arch came to symbolize that revitalization effort.

The arch draws four million visitors annually and its impact on the local economy is substantial. Nevertheless, one attraction, however monumental, cannot be an anchor for a city that has been in serious decline. In the half century since the completion of the arch, the city's population decreased from 750,000 to 318,000, and St. Louis, once America's tenth-largest city, is now fifty-eighth in size. Across the river, the fragile remains of Cahokia offer a sobering reminder of the rise and fall of great civilizations.

WEBSITES
Cahokia, www.cahokiamounds.org
Gateway Arch, www.gatewayarch.org or www.nps.gov/jeff

NEARBY PLACES
Missouri History Museum, www.mohistory.org
Saint Louis Art Museum, www.slam.org
Cathedral Basilica of Saint Louis, www.cathedralstl.org
Anheuser-Busch Brewery, www.budweisertours.com
Scott Joplin House, http://www.mostateparks.com/park/scott-joplin
    -house-state-historic-site

3

MESA VERDE
CORTEZ, COLORADO

Cliff Palace

The early inhabitants of our country sustained a vibrant culture in a harsh and unforgiving environment. The spectacular ruins of the Ancestral Puebloan people (formerly known as Anasazi) in Mesa Verde and beyond its borders continue to puzzle experts. How did an ancient civilization build a complex society and survive for hundreds of years in the mesa's semiarid landscape without metal tools, wagons, or horses? What caused them to retreat to cliff dwellings dug into the sides of canyons? Why did they disappear suddenly from this land? Where did they go?

Mesa Verde, Spanish for "green table," is located in the Four Corners region in southwestern Colorado at its border with Utah, New Mexico, and Arizona. The mesa is a sandstone and shale formation that reaches a height of 2,000 feet above the surrounding plain and an elevation of 6,000 to 8,500 feet above sea level. It measures twenty-five miles across on the north side and slopes to the south for eight miles to a height of 1,000 feet. Canyons formed by ancient drainages divide the mesa into smaller sections that run north to south. The Puebloans lived here for seven hundred years. Through evidence of their architecture, agriculture, crafts, and religion, archaeologists have identified several major periods of settlement. The Basket Maker period, from around 550 to 750, marked a transition when migrants from nearby sites colonized the mesa and created stable settlements based on farming. The Basket Makers first lived in pit houses dug a few feet belowground, with roofs supported by wooden poles. They made pottery and adopted new technologies such as the bow and arrow for hunting. By 800, the Puebloan period was marked by houses built aboveground with long walls made of adobe—mud bricks—and a *kiva* that evolved over time into a ceremonial room featuring a small hole, or *sipapu*, in the floor through which, the Puebloans believed, the spirits of ancestors entered and left the present world. Beginning around 1050, Pueblo buildings changed from adobe to masonry construction, and some became quite large—two and three stories tall with fifty or more rooms arranged around a central plaza. These *pueblos* (the Spanish word for "villages") are extraordinary examples of masonry construction and town planning.

On the fertile fields of the mesa, the Puebloans grew corn, squash, and beans. They raised turkeys and hunted deer, rabbits, and squirrels. They traded with neighboring peoples to the south in Chaco Canyon and to the west along the Pacific Coast. Their religion centered on the agricultural cycle and astronomical observations as well as a belief in personal connections with the spirit world.

The most fascinating chapter of Mesa Verde's history came at the end of the Classic Period—1100 to 1300—and lasted only a hundred years. Puebloans began building dwellings in alcoves under overhanging canyon cliffs, possibly to accommodate a growing population and to offer protection from a harsh climate and potential enemies. Using sandstone, bricks, and mortar, they built more than 600 cliff dwellings. While most of these were 1 and 2 rooms, there were several multiroom dwellings such as Spruce Tree House (130 rooms), Long House (150 rooms), and Balcony House (40 rooms). The best-known cliff dwelling is Cliff Palace, a mini-city consisting of 150 rooms, 21 ceremonial kivas, and 25 to 30 living quarters housing around 100 to 120 people.

By 1225, the population of Mesa Verde had reached more than three thousand. Yet within a few decades of building the cliff dwellings, the Ancestral Puebloans abandoned the mesa. The reasons for this sudden migration are still a matter of speculation, since they left behind no written records. Scientists have concluded that several factors—the depletion of soil and other resources, increased warfare, climate change, and a prolonged drought at the end of the thirteenth century—forced their migration south from Mesa Verde to warmer locations in the Rio Grande region and Arizona.

Today, the descendants of the Puebloans—the Hopi in Arizona and people of the nineteen pueblos in northern New Mexico, including Taos, Acoma, and Zuni—reflect the cultural heritage of the Ancestral Puebloans. They maintain a strong connection to ancestors who lived before European settlement, survived massacres and epidemics, and preserved forms of self-governance and living traditions in their contemporary lives. This legacy is also sustained in the beautiful baskets, pottery, and weaving displayed in museums and prized by collectors throughout the world.

For nearly six hundred years, the civilization created by the Puebloans was largely invisible and unknown. In the late nineteenth century, geologists and prospectors noticed the cliff dwellings, and photographer William Henry Jackson produced the first images of these sites in 1874. In 1888, members of the Wetherill family, ranchers in nearby Mancos Valley, explored Cliff Palace and other ruins. Over the next five years, they entered almost two hundred cliff dwellings and assembled enormous artifact collections, which they sold to the Colorado Historical Society. News of their discoveries attracted treasure hunters, who looted many significant sites.

While the Wetherill family could be accused of exploiting Mesa Verde for their own profit, they deserve credit for recognizing the need for documentation and preservation. In 1889 and 1890, they guided Frederick Chapin, a mountaineer and author, through the ruins. His book *The Land of the Cliff-Dwellers* (1892) introduced Mesa Verde to the world. They also guided a Swedish scientist, Gustaf Nordenskiöld, who systematically excavated, documented, and photographed several sites, exporting some six hundred Mesa Verde objects to the National Museum of Helsinki. The Wetherills later joined activists including Virginia McClurg and the Colorado Cliff Dwellings Association as advocates for protection of Mesa Verde. Their efforts culminated in passage of the Antiquities Act (1906) and the creation of a national park, America's first cultural park. In 1978, Mesa Verde received designation as a World Heritage Site. Today, visitors can explore cliff dwellings, pueblos, and pit houses. The Chapin Museum houses an excellent collection and dioramas created by the Civilian Conservation Corps (CCC) in the 1930s, an example of the contributions the CCC made to every national park.

The National Park Service, universities, and foundations sponsor research at many of Mesa Verde's 4,700 sites. The nearby Crow Canyon Archaeological Research Center conducts surveys, excavations, and field schools at Ancestral sites on the plains surrounding the mesa and this research links the Mesa Verde region to Chaco Canyon, another World Heritage Site, which lies farther south. Combining scholarship and innovative techniques, these institutions continue to expand our knowledge.

WEBSITES
Mesa Verde National Park, www.nps.gov/meve
History Colorado, www.historycolorado.org

NEARBY PLACES
Chaco Culture National Historical Park, www.nps.gov/chcu
Crow Canyon Archaeological Research Center, www.crowcanyon.org
Anasazi Heritage Center, www.blm.gov/co/st/en/fo/ahc.html

4

THE PALACE OF
THE GOVERNORS
SANTA FE, NEW MEXICO

Palace of the Governors

Beginning a decade before the Pilgrims landed at Plymouth Rock, and continuing for four centuries into the present, the thick adobe walls of the Palace of the Governors sheltered succeeding waves of Spanish colonial governors and military leaders, Pueblo Indian rebels, Mexican officers, U.S. territorial governors, and Confederate troops during the Civil War as well as artists, writers, curators, historians, art lovers, and tourists. Located on Santa Fe's historic plaza, the palace also served as headquarters for the Museum of New Mexico, which promoted economic revival based on tourism in the twentieth century.

The Spanish colonization of what is now New Mexico began in 1598 when Juan de Oñate led a small force of soldiers, their families, and a few Franciscan priests in search of silver mines and Indian converts. The Spanish called the Indians Pueblos because they lived in villages. The people in one of these villages, called Acoma, resisted Oñate's demands for food and blankets. Oñate ordered a brutal reprisal, burning the village, killing half its population, and taking the rest prisoner. He gave children away to priests, enslaved adults, and cut off the feet of several Indian men. The destruction of Acoma pueblo in 1599 foreshadowed the course of New Mexico's history for the next century.

The Spanish never found silver, but the Franciscans converted thousands of pueblo natives to Christianity. They persuaded Spain's monarchy to appoint a new governor, create a royal colony, and establish a new capital. In 1609, Governor Pedro de Peralta selected a site at the foot of the Sangre de Cristo Mountains following guidelines known as the Laws of the Indies, issued by King Philip II in 1573, which governed all Spanish settlements in the New World. Peralta named the town Villa de Santa

Fé and established a town council, a *cabildo*, with authority to allocate space for public buildings, homes and farms, and, most important, to manage water distribution from the nearby Santa Fe River. Peralta's residence and council headquarters was the Palace of the Governors on the north side of the town square, or *plaza*. Construction of the palace began in 1610 and continued for almost a decade. Despite many changes in size and appearance over the centuries, the palace remains the oldest continuously occupied public building in the United States.

Spanish New Mexico in the seventeenth century consisted of Santa Fe and around fifty Franciscan missions. The Spanish sustained their colony by exploiting their Indian neighbors: requiring contributions of corn, cloth, and hides; enslaving local Indians; and sending warriors captured in battle as slave labor for Mexican mines. Converting Indians to Christianity remained an important goal but the need for their labor became a necessity. However, the Pueblo Indian workforce was declining, the result of smallpox epidemics in the 1630s, periodic droughts, and warfare with raiding Apaches. As their situation became more desperate, the Indians tried to revive ancient religious practices. In 1675, Franciscan priests pressed the government to arrest Native shamans, or priests. They executed three religious leaders and tortured several more. Indian warriors poured into Santa Fe and secured release of their priests.

One religious leader, Po'pay, spent the next five years at Okhe Pueblo near Taos organizing a rebellion—the only successful Native revolt in American history. In August 1680, his coalition of six thousand warriors from at least seven tribes launched a surprise attack on Santa Fe and thirty-three Catholic missions. For nine days, Po'pay's forces laid siege to the Palace of the Governors, trapping Governor Antonio de Otermín and two hundred Spanish soldiers and their families. When the Indians cut off the water supply, Otermín's party withdrew and fled south to what is now Juarez, Mexico. The rebels had killed a quarter of the colony's Spanish population, including twenty-one priests. For the next twelve years, the Pueblos occupied Santa Fe and tried to destroy vestiges of Spanish culture. Their triumph was short-lived; conflicts within their leadership weakened the new regime. In 1692, a Spanish captain, Diego de Vargas, began a campaign that ultimately restored Spain's colonial power.

An era of coexistence that lasted for more than a century followed Po'pay's Pueblo Revolt. The Spanish reduced their demands on the Pueblos and concentrated on building Santa Fe as a commercial center and defending its northern frontier. With its location on El Camino Réal de Tierra Adentro (the Royal Road), the town and surrounding area attracted a large Spanish population.

Early in the nineteenth century, Spain's imperial power faded. The Mexican War of Independence that ended in 1821 created the republic of Mexico. In that year, the Santa Fe Trail opened, bringing trade and settlers from America's heartland to Santa Fe's main plaza. The Mexican War of 1846–48 resulted in the transfer of most of New Mexico to the United States. Although Santa Fe remained the territorial capital, its economy suffered when the Atchison, Topeka and Santa Fe Railway selected a route in 1880 that bypassed the city. When New Mexico entered the union as a state in 1912, Santa Fe was a city in decline.

Twentieth-century tourism rescued Santa Fe's economy. The vision and leadership for this transformation came from the Museum of New Mexico, founded by Edgar L. Hewett in 1909. In 1912, Hewett and his associates wrote a city plan influenced by the national City Beautiful movement. They recommended adopting the historic architecture of the Indians and Spanish and even renaming streets with Spanish names to honor this tradition. The Pueblo-Spanish style featured buildings that were low and long with flat roofs, adobe walls and buttresses, *portales* (porches), casement windows, projecting wooden *vigas* (beams), and *canales* (roof drains). The first new building to adopt this style was the Museum of Fine Arts (1917), designed by Isaac Rapp, which collected and presented the work of a growing art colony. Architect John Gaw Meem popularized the Santa Fe style in the La Fonda Hotel (1927) and the Laboratory of Anthropology (1930).

The Palace of the Governors, restored in the Pueblo-Spanish style in

1909–1913, symbolizes Santa Fe's revival. Archaeological research of the palace complex as well as the pueblo and presidio has contributed significant evidence of Spanish and Pueblo occupations. Today, the palace occupies a much smaller footprint and is part of the New Mexico History Museum that recently expanded into a new building. Its plaza *portal* hosts a daily marketplace for Native American artists. Other downtown museums and those on the Old Santa Fe Trail south of the plaza display collections of New Mexican fine arts, Indian arts and culture, Hispanic colonial arts, and international folk art. In 1997, the Georgia O'Keeffe Museum opened near the plaza. The Santa Fe Opera, the International Folk Market, and Site Santa Fe have transformed the city into a major arts center.

While the Pueblos and Spanish did not achieve military or political dominance, their cultural heritage has endured, a blend of an authentic, sometimes harsh reality and a spirited romantic revival. Surrounding Santa Fe is the stunning landscape of the high desert, immortalized by writers and artists for its light and natural beauty. D. H. Lawrence: "The moment I saw the brilliant, proud morning shine high up over the deserts of Santa Fe, something stood still in my soul. . . . In the magnificent fierce morning of New Mexico one sprang awake, a new part of the soul woke up suddenly, and the old world gave way to the new."

WEBSITES
Palace of the Governors, www.palaceofthegovernors.org
New Mexico History Museum, www.nmhistorymuseum.org
Museum of New Mexico, www.museumofnewmexico.org
Georgia O'Keeffe Museum, www.okeeffemuseum.org

NEARBY PLACES
Acoma Pueblo, www.puebloofacoma.org
Bandelier National Monument, www.nps.gov/band

5

WITCH TRIALS

SALEM, MASSACHUSETTS

TINA KOUTSOS-JORDAN

Salem Witch Trials Memorial

TINA KOUTSOS-JORDAN

Detail of Salem Witch Trials Memorial

The town of Salem derives its name from words in Hebrew (*shalom*) and Arabic (*salaam*) that mean "peace." But in 1692, this seaport village fifteen miles north of Boston was anything but peaceful. Mass hysteria, fueled by fear, prejudice, and ignorance, swept through Salem and neighboring towns. Within a year, it was over. Yet the deep scars of this dark episode have persisted for three centuries.

In seventeenth-century New England, religious faith dominated daily life. People accepted the presence of God in their personal lives. They also believed that the devil and his agents could appear in the form of witches and otherworldly spirits. In January 1692, two girls living in the household of Samuel Parris, a Puritan minister from Salem Village (now Danvers), began having convulsions and screaming fits. Other girls in the community soon exhibited the same behavior. Doctors who examined the girls found no medical explanation and speculated that a satanic force—the devil—caused their behavior. The girls told of spending time with an enslaved woman, Tituba, who entertained them with tales of magic and the supernatural from her native Barbados. The girls named Tituba and two other women as witches. On March 1, local justices examined the women and the Salem witch hunt began. Within two months, new accusations put fifty more people in the Salem Village jail.

In May, a new governor, Sir William Phips, arrived in Boston. Hearing reports of a witch conspiracy in Salem, he appointed Lieutenant Governor William Stoughton to lead a Court of Oyer and Terminer, meaning "to hear and decide," to conduct the witchcraft trials. The court's procedures created at least two problems. First, it allowed "spectral evidence," testimony supported only by visions and dreams, a decision that encouraged exaggeration and outright fraud. Second, the court prosecuted only those who denied the accusations rather than those who confessed and accused others.

The charges and countercharges escalated and divided the community and families. Husbands accused wives, daughters named parents and grandparents. Women, many of them elderly, poor, widowed, or with criminal records, were most frequently accused, but several men also became targets. Nearly two hundred people filled local jails for weeks at a time. Several died awaiting trial.

The special court tried fifty-nine people and convicted thirty-one from Salem Town (present-day Salem), Salem Village, and other towns. Nineteen people—fourteen women and five men—were hanged because they refused to confess. The first person executed was Bridget Bishop on June 10. Three more public hangings took place on July 19, August 19, and September 22. A mob mentality prevailed at the trials. For example, the court found Rebecca Nurse not guilty but, under pressure from spectators, reversed its decision and sentenced her to death. One man, Giles Corey, eighty years old, refused to enter a plea and suffered a punishment known as *peine forte et dure*—the only such execution in American history. For two days, he lay naked in a pit while men lowered heavy stones on a board pressed against his chest until he died.

The Salem trials attracted criticism from the beginning. One judge resigned from the court in protest after the first trial. Several people circulated petitions supporting individual defendants. The most prominent critic was Increase Mather, a minister and former president of Harvard University. His son, Cotton Mather, had expressed his belief in witchcraft and supported the trials. His father agreed that witches existed, but he adamantly opposed the abuses of the special court. "It were better that ten witches should escape," he wrote, "than that one innocent person should be condemned."

By late October, criticism surrounding the trials persuaded Governor Phips to dissolve the special court. He created a Superior Court to review the remaining cases and this court completed its work in May

1693 with no additional convictions. The tragic and tumultuous year of the Salem witch hunt was over but never forgotten. Several judges and jury members apologized for their actions. In 1711, a colonial court reversed the convictions and provided compensation to survivors and the families of women and men who went to the gallows.

Historians trying to understand the witch hunt point to a number of issues—Indian wars, smallpox epidemics, political instability, rivalries within local families and congregations, and conflicts between rich and poor—as contributing to the tensions that shook Salem in 1692. The trials also revealed the prejudice against women in colonial society. The entire episode reflected the transition under way as the Age of Faith receded and the Age of Enlightenment began.

The literary legacy of the Salem witch hunt is especially robust. From Henry Wadsworth Longfellow's poem about Giles Corey to Nathaniel Hawthorne, a descendant of a witch trial judge, to Arthur Miller, whose play *The Crucible* (1953) used the trials as a parable for anti-Communist investigations known as McCarthyism, the witch hunt has inspired writers to examine the irrational forces that can, at any moment, undermine basic principles of justice.

In Salem today, at sites like the Jonathan Corwin House (now known as the Witch House Museum) and the Salem Witch Museum, the witch trials dominate public memory, overshadowing other aspects of Salem's history. Salem was, in fact, a prosperous maritime community, a story well told at the Maritime National Historic Site. Beautiful mansions like those found on historic Chestnut Street reflect the success of merchants and shipowners. Along the waterfront, the House of the Seven Gables is an example of the historic preservation movement. One of America's best museums, the Peabody Essex Museum, exhibits art and artifacts from around the world and maintains a library that houses the Salem Witch Trial papers, the most authoritative collection on the subject.

The Witch Trials Memorial, designed by James Cutler and Maggie Smith and dedicated in 1992, is a short walk from the museum. The memorial consists of twenty granite benches with the names of the victims and the dates of their executions. The entrance to the park contains paving stones carved with the victims' final words. Black locusts represent the trees from which they were hanged. At the dedication ceremony, Elie Wiesel, a Holocaust survivor, spoke of remembering "those who died rather than tell a lie to save their lives."

There is another memorial in Danvers, where the witch hunt began. Nearby is the Rebecca Nurse Homestead. Public tours include the home and a family cemetery with a marble monument inscribed with a poem by John Greenleaf Whittier that reads:

> *O Christian Martyr*
> *who for Truth could die*
> *When all about thee*
> *owned the hideous lie!*
> *The world redeemed*
> *from superstitions sway*
> *Is breathing freer*
> *for thy sake to-day.*

WEBSITES

Salem Witch Museum, www.salemwitchmuseum.com
Salem Witch Trials Memorial, www.salemweb.com/memorial/
memorial.shtml

NEARBY PLACES

Jonathan Corwin House, www.witchhouse.info
Salem Maritime National Historic Site, www.nps.gov/sama
Peabody Essex Museum, www.pem.org
The House of the Seven Gables, www.7gables.org
The Rebecca Nurse Homestead, www.rebeccanurse.org

6

BOUNDARY LINE

NEW CASTLE, DELAWARE

New Castle Court House

A small town in one of America's smallest states, New Castle has a large historical significance, connected to international conflicts, interstate rivalries, independence, the Underground Railroad, and our country's most famous boundary, the Mason-Dixon Line.

In the seventeenth century, the Delaware Valley was the setting for the competing claims of three European nations—the Netherlands, Sweden, and England. The Dutch had explored and claimed these lands as New Netherlands in 1609, a claim that extended as far north as the Hudson River Valley. Despite the Dutch presence, Swedish and Finnish settlers established a fort near present-day Wilmington, Delaware, in 1638 and called their colony New Sweden. To control trade routes and prevent the Swedes from moving their settlements up the Delaware River, the Dutch built Fort Casimir, in 1651, near present-day New Castle. The Swedes captured this fort and renamed it Fort Trinity in 1654. The next year, the Dutch launched a counterassault, took back the fort, and laid out a town called New Amstel.

During this same period, England's growing empire surrounded the Dutch colonies—to the north in New England and to the south in Virginia and the Carolinas. After 1660, England confronted the Dutch and pressured them to abandon their American holdings. In 1664, Peter Stuyvesant, governor of New Netherlands, watched from a fortress in New Amsterdam (now lower Manhattan) as a fleet of English ships, under the command of the Duke of York, sailed up the Hudson River. Offering only token resistance, Stuyvesant surrendered the Dutch territories and England divided New Netherlands into the colonies of New York, New Jersey, and Delaware. New Amstel was renamed New Castle and made the seat of regional government.

The power struggle over New Castle and Delaware entered a new phase. When King Charles II granted a charter to William Penn to establish the new colony of Pennsylvania in 1681, Penn requested that the southeastern boundary of his colony include access to the Atlantic Ocean. The Duke of York, who retained administrative control over the former Dutch colonies, granted this request, and Penn landed at New Castle on his first visit to America on October 27, 1682.

People in New Castle and two neighboring counties, many of them of Dutch descent, resented Penn's conservative Quaker government based in Philadelphia. When Penn issued a new constitution in 1701, known as the Charter of Privileges, the three counties secured the right to establish their own assembly. Although the two colonies continued under a single governor, an independent legislature, based in New Castle, became Delaware's governing body. The New Castle Court House, built in 1732 and one of America's oldest public buildings, was the site where Delaware's legislature debated and declared independence from Great Britain and Pennsylvania in June 1776.

A decade before the American Revolution, the New Castle Court House became associated with the Mason-Dixon Line, a line created not to separate North and South but to settle a boundary dispute between Pennsylvania and Maryland. In 1763 the two feuding colonies agreed to establish boundaries prescribed by a British court and a boundary commission that recommended using the cupola of the New Castle Court House as the starting point for a twelve-mile arc forming part of Pennsylvania's southern boundary. They hired two experts, Charles Mason, an astronomer at the Royal Society in Greenwich, and Jeremiah Dixon, a surveyor from Durham County, England. For four years, they braved rugged terrain, harsh climate, and hostile whites and Indians to mark the 83-mile boundary between Maryland and Delaware and the 233-mile boundary between Maryland and Pennsylvania. Using the stars, a few surveying instruments, and a library of technical journals, they established a line so accurate that, according to modern surveying techniques, it is off course by only an inch in some places and never more than eight hundred feet. They imported huge blocks of limestone from England, weighing between three hundred and five hundred pounds, and placed them at mile intervals with a *P* for Pennsylvania and an *M* for Maryland engraved on each side. Every five miles, they placed stones engraved with the coats of arms of the Calvert and Penn families.

This engineering landmark of the eighteenth century gained new relevance in the nineteenth as the reference point in the Missouri Compromise of 1820, which divided free and slave states. The line's fame rivals that of the equator and the Maginot Line. Today, dedicated hikers can still find many of the stone markers of this unlikely symbol of freedom.

In 1848, New Castle's main courtroom was the scene of a landmark trial involving the Underground Railroad. Thomas Garrett and John Hunn, two prominent "stationmasters," were accused of violating federal law for their roles in assisting the Hawkins family of Maryland to escape from slavery. Garrett is credited with conducting more than 2,700 fugitives to freedom, and Harriet Beecher Stowe used his story to create the abolitionist Simeon Halliday in *Uncle Tom's Cabin.* Garrett and Hunn were convicted and fined in trials presided over by Roger B. Taney, the chief justice of the U.S. Supreme Court, who later wrote the infamous Dred Scott decision, in 1857, that found Congress could not regulate slavery in U.S. territories and denied African Americans, free or enslaved, any rights under the Constitution.

Today at the New Castle Court House, visitors can learn about the Hawkins family and the Garrett trial and begin a self-guided tour of New Castle's beautifully preserved historic district that includes the village green laid out by the Dutch; the remains of fortifications; more than a hundred colonial-, federal-, and Victorian-style buildings; and the site where William Penn, arriving aboard the ship *Welcome*, landed. In Wilmington, six miles north, there are reminders of Swedish heritage at the New Sweden Centre and at the *Kalmar Nyckel*, the reconstructed flagship of Dutch colonial governor Peter Minuit and later a Swedish vessel. Visitors to Wilmington must see the extraordinary collections, gardens, and archives of Winterthur and the Hagley Museum & Library, legacies of the du Pont family, who emigrated from France in 1800, another example of this region's multicultural heritage.

WEBSITE
New Castle Court House Museum, www.history.delaware.gov
    /museums/ncch/ncch_main.shtml

NEARBY PLACES
New Castle Historical Society, www.newcastlehistory.org
Hagley Museum, www.hagley.org
Winterthur, www.winterthur.org
The Dutch House, www.newcastlehistory.org/houses/dutch.html
New Sweden Centre, www.colonialnewsweden.org

7

FORKS OF THE OHIO

PITTSBURGH, PENNSYLVANIA

Forks of the Ohio

In the eighteenth century, the Forks of the Ohio—where the Allegheny and Monongahela Rivers join to form the Ohio River—was a site of critical strategic importance as Britain and France clashed over control of their colonial empires in North America. This conflict, known in American history as the French and Indian War, was actually part of a worldwide Seven Years' War that engulfed Europe, Asia, Africa, and the Caribbean. In addition, this period was a turning point in the early careers of two American founders—George Washington and Benjamin Franklin.

Washington was a young officer in the Virginia militia when he led an expedition into the Ohio River Valley in 1753 to dislodge the French, who had built four forts from Lake Erie to Fort Duquesne in what is now Pittsburgh. His mission failed and he suffered a devastating defeat by the French and their Indian allies at Fort Necessity in July 1754. A year later, Washington joined General Edward Braddock, who commanded a force of two thousand English and Virginia soldiers determined to capture Fort Duquesne. With Franklin arranging supplies and wagons, Braddock's army built a road several hundred miles through woods and over mountaintops. Before they reached the Forks, a small band of French and Indians staged a surprise attack, killed Braddock, and left half the British army dead or wounded. In 1756, Britain declared war on France and the Seven Years' War began.

Braddock's replacements renewed their campaign to drive the French from their strongholds in Canada, Lake Champlain, and the Ohio River Valley. In 1758, General John Forbes led an expedition across Pennsylvania to capture Fort Duquesne. He constructed a new road and built forts at Bedford and Ligonier along the route. By the time he reached Fort Duquesne, the French had destroyed the fort and retreated. Forbes built a new fort and named it for William Pitt, the minister responsible for directing Britain's war effort. The following year, Britain, led by General James Wolfe, defeated the French at the Battle of Quebec, effectively ending France's presence as a colonial power in North America.

The Treaty of Paris, signed in February 1763, codified Britain's victory in the Seven Years' War. In addition to giving up control of Canada and lands east of the Mississippi River, France also accepted the British as an economic power in India and the Caribbean. France's ally, Spain, ceded control of Florida. As a result, Great Britain emerged as the greatest European power since the Roman Empire.

Britain's dominant position in North America antagonized several Indian tribes who did not welcome military occupation or the expansion of white settlement west of the Appalachian Mountains in spite of treaties and royal proclamations. The strongest Indian challenge came from a confederation of tribes led by Pontiac, an Ottawan chief from the Lake Michigan region. In the spring of 1763, Pontiac's forces captured nine British forts and his allies—Delawares and Shawnees—surrounded Fort Pitt. The situation was critical and British commander in chief Jeffrey Amherst ordered a relief squadron of five hundred troops under Colonel Henry Bouquet to break the Indian siege. At one point, Amherst was desperate and instructed Bouquet to use germ warfare. "Could it not be contrived," he wrote, "to send the smallpox among the disaffected tribes of Indians? We must on this occasion use every stratagem in our power to reduce them." Bouquet replied, "I will try to inoculate the bastards with some blankets . . . and take care not to get the disease myself." In fact, officers at Fort Pitt had already used this tactic with no apparent effect. Bouquet broke the siege with a dramatic if more conventional victory in the Battle of Bushy Run on August 5–6, 1763. Pontiac's Rebellion ended with a peace treaty in 1766.

Several historic sites preserve the legacy of the French and Indian War in western Pennsylvania. Fort Necessity National Battlefield, Fort

Ligonier, and Bushy Run Battlefield are all located within an hour's drive of downtown Pittsburgh. The Fort Pitt Block House, a small brick structure built in 1764, is the oldest building in Pittsburgh. Remarkably, the Block House survived as Pittsburgh grew from a commercial port city to an industrial powerhouse. In 1894, philanthropist Mary Schenley donated the Block House to the Daughters of the American Revolution, who, in spite of the powerful opposition of Henry Clay Frick and the Pennsylvania Railroad, managed to secure its preservation. After World War II, as Pittsburgh launched an urban renaissance, the Block House and the archaeological remains of Fort Pitt became part of Point State Park along with the Fort Pitt Museum.

The history of Pittsburgh and western Pennsylvania is on display at the Heinz History Center. Located in a former ice plant in the Strip District, the center also manages the Fort Pitt Museum and Meadowcroft Rockshelter and Historic Village, a prehistoric site with twenty periods of human occupation dating back sixteen thousand years. Artifacts from Meadowcroft caused scientists to revise their estimates of when settlement in North America first occurred. These discoveries and the evidence of Native people who have continuously lived in this region confirm the pivotal role of the Ohio River Valley long before the exploits of young George Washington sparked a conflict that became a world war.

WEBSITES
Fort Pitt Museum, www.heinzhistorycenter.org/fort-pitt
Heinz History Center, www.heinzhistorycenter.org

NEARBY PLACES
Bushy Run Battlefield, www.bushyrunbattlefield.com
Fort Ligonier, www.fortligonier.org
Fort Necessity National Battlefield, www.nps.gov/fone

8

FREEDOM TRAIL

BOSTON, MASSACHUSETTS

Faneuil Hall

For more than a decade before the Continental Congress adopted the Declaration of Independence in Philadelphia in July 1776, Boston was the center of colonial resistance against British rule. A walking tour of Revolutionary War sites—the Freedom Trail—provides dramatic evidence of the extraordinary events that set the stage for the conflict that finally ended with the British surrender in Yorktown, Virginia, in 1781 and the Treaty of Paris of 1783.

The Freedom Trail is a 2.5-mile route that begins in downtown Boston, crosses the Charles River, and ends at the Bunker Hill Monument. This route includes sixteen sites of events ingrained in America's collective memory, such as the Boston Massacre, the Boston Tea Party, Paul Revere's Ride, and the Battle of Bunker Hill. The trail starts at the Boston Common, where Bostonians celebrated the repeal of the Stamp Act in 1765 and where the British headquartered during their occupation of the city from 1768 to 1776.

The first clash between these troops and city residents came on March 5, 1770. A petty argument between a British soldier and a barber's apprentice sparked a confrontation between a jeering mob and nine British soldiers near the Old State House, the center of the royal government. Within minutes, the troops fired on the boisterous crowd, killing five men—including an African American, Crispus Attucks—and wounding several more. The Boston Massacre provoked protests and meetings in which Samuel Adams and others called for the withdrawal of British troops and for independence for the American colonies.

John Adams, Samuel's cousin, took a more moderate approach. He agreed to defend the British soldiers who had been charged with murder, won their acquittal, and emerged as a major spokesman for Boston and Massachusetts. His legal training, powerful intellect, and riveting speaking style made him an ideal leader for the American cause. As tensions grew in the 1770s, Adams accepted that American independence was inevitable. He represented Massachusetts at both Continental Congresses in Philadelphia, and coauthored the Declaration of Independence with Thomas Jefferson and Benjamin Franklin. He served as ambassador to England in the 1780s, then as first vice president and second president of the United States. Few people in our history can match his superb record of public service during America's formative years.

Nearly four years after the Boston Massacre, another protest—the Boston Tea Party—became the defining moment of colonial resistance. This was a planned event, organized by a group called the Sons of Liberty in response to a British law that gave a monopoly on the sale of tea to the East India Company, a corporation closely aligned with the British governor of Massachusetts. On the evening of December 16, 1773, around 120 men and boys dressed as Mohawk Indians marched from the Old South Meeting House to Griffin's Wharf, boarded three ships, and threw 342 chests of tea into Boston Harbor. The loss to the East India Company was the equivalent of $1 million today. As punishment for the Tea Party, the British closed Boston's port, restricted ferries, and abolished local government.

The center of the Tea Party protest and other public meetings was Faneuil Hall, a market and meeting place built in 1742. Colonists began gathering at this site in the 1760s to protest various British laws and to debate political issues. The funeral service for the Boston Massacre victims took place there and the Boston Committee of Correspondence, organized to communicate events and opinions to other towns and colonies, started there. Even after the revolution, Faneuil Hall continued to function as a place for public debate. Throughout the nineteenth century, advocates for the abolition of slavery, woman suffrage, and temperance rallied for their causes at the hall.

Highways and parkland now cover the actual site of the Boston Tea

Party; however, other stops on the Freedom Trail include buildings that are rare survivors of the Revolutionary period. The Paul Revere House on North Square is one of those places. Revere and his large family lived here while he worked as a silversmith in a nearby shop. A true hero of the American cause for liberty, he joined Boston's political groups and promoted the resistance movement by producing copper plate engravings of the Boston Massacre and other events. He also served as a messenger for the Committee of Correspondence, riding thousands of miles to bring news of events in Boston and alerting colonists of British activities there. His most celebrated ride was on April 18, 1775, to Lexington and, the next day, to Concord. The warnings by Revere, sixteen-year-old Sybil Ludington, and other riders about advancing British troops gave the Americans time to prepare and win significant victories. The American Revolution had begun!

For the next year, the conflict continued around Boston. The British victory at Breed's Hill in Charlestown came only after the British sustained heavy losses. The Bunker Hill Monument, another stop on the Freedom Trail, commemorates this major battle. George Washington arrived in July 1775 and organized a siege that cut British access to supplies and reinforcements. On March 17, 1776, they abandoned Boston and shifted their attention to strategic targets in New York, New Jersey, and Pennsylvania.

There are two more noteworthy stops on the Freedom Trail that commemorate later wars. The first is the USS *Constitution*, the warship launched in 1797 that protected merchant ships from North African pirates and later fought in significant victories against British ships in the War of 1812. The second is the Shaw Memorial, across from the Massachusetts State House. Designed by Augustus Saint-Gaudens and dedicated in 1897, the memorial commemorates the leadership of Colonel Robert Gould Shaw and the courageous service of African American troops in the 54th Massachusetts Regiment in the Civil War.

The history of the Freedom Trail itself is a good example of historic preservation. In 1951, a journalist, Bill Schofield, and a local historian,

Bob Winn, started a campaign to recognize Boston's rich concentration of historic places with plaques, brochures, and memorials. By 1958, the trail had attracted thousands of visitors, and a local businessman, Dick Berenson, proposed painting a red line to help visitors follow the trail. This was done and the red line remains today. Information centers, gift shops, and guided tours followed. Several million people each year explore the Freedom Trail and discover the remarkable stories of people seeking and fighting for the liberty to govern themselves.

WEBSITES
The Freedom Trail, www.thefreedomtrail.org
USS *Constitution*, www.ussconstitutionmuseum.org
Robert Gould Shaw and Massachusetts 54th Regiment Memorial,
    www.nps.gov/boaf/learn/historyculture/shaw.htm
Lexington and Concord, www.nps.gov/mima

NEARBY PLACES
Walden Pond State Reservation, www.mass.gov/eea/agencies/dcr
    /massparks/region-north/walden-pond-state-reservation.html
The Mary Baker Eddy Library, www.marybakereddylibrary.org
Museum of Fine Arts, Boston, www.mfa.org
Adams National Historical Park, www.nps.gov/adam

9

THE LIBERTY BELL

PHILADELPHIA, PENNSYLVANIA

The Liberty Bell

In 1751, Pennsylvania celebrated the fiftieth anniversary of its colonial constitution by commissioning a new bell for the tower of its assembly hall in Philadelphia. A local foundry, Pass and Stow, produced a 2,080-pound bell inscribed with the biblical quotation "Proclaim LIBERTY throughout all the land unto all the inhabitants thereof" (Lev. 25:10). Today, it is called the Liberty Bell.

The colonial constitution, called the Charter of Privileges and signed by William Penn in 1701, was a milestone in colonial governance. Although Penn had a royal charter for the colony named in honor of his father in 1681, he faced constant opposition from various constituencies. The Charter of Privileges was his third attempt to give Pennsylvanians basic rights while he retained final authority. The charter established a permanent legislature with power to elect its own leadership and to propose amendments for Penn's approval. Most significantly, Penn asserted the rights of individual citizens to practice their own religious faith "without molestation and interference" by the government. He stated this commitment clearly in the charter's final section:

> . . . because the happiness of Mankind Depends So much upon the Enjoying of Libertie of theire Consciences . . . that the first Article of this Charter Relateing to Liberty of Conscience . . . shall be kept and remaine without any Alteration Inviolably for ever.

The original charter survives today at the American Philosophical Society, located just two blocks from the Liberty Bell Pavilion in

Independence National Historical Park. Founded by Benjamin Franklin in 1743, the society reflected Philadelphia's significant role as America's intellectual capital in the eighteenth century. Scientists and scholars were members, as were doctors, lawyers, clergymen, and merchants, and the society published papers, sponsored scientific investigations, and collected specimens and objects. Before there was the Library of Congress (1800) or the Smithsonian Institution (1846), the society was a national center of research and learning.

Franklin's contributions to Philadelphia and the nation were extraordinary. He achieved success as a printer and published newspapers, government documents, paper money, and *Poor Richard's Almanac*, an annual pamphlet containing scientific information and practical advice. At age forty-two, he retired and devoted himself to practical applications of science—discovering electricity, inventing bifocal glasses, and promoting Daylight Saving Time—and to civic institutions, including a firefighting company, an insurance association, a public library, and an academy that later became the University of Pennsylvania. Although he initially favored preserving America's ties to Great Britain, he became an enthusiastic supporter of independence, serving as a delegate to the Second Continental Congress (1775), coauthor of the Declaration of Independence, ambassador to France during the revolution, and a delegate to the Constitutional Convention (1787).

During Franklin's lifetime, the building now called Independence Hall was known as the Pennsylvania State House, and what we call the Liberty Bell was simply the State House Bell that rang to announce when the assembly was in session or when important public announcements would be read. The State House, designed by Andrew Hamilton and constructed in various stages between 1732 and 1756, is now (as Independence Hall) recognized as a World Heritage Site. The association of this building with both the Declaration of Independence and the U.S. Constitution and its service as a home of our national government make it an enduring symbol of democracy.

Nevertheless, there was a period in the early nineteenth century—after the capital moved to Washington, D.C.—when the State House clock tower was crumbling and various renovations threatened its historic integrity. A well-publicized visit by the Marquis de Lafayette in 1824 brought attention to the deteriorated condition of the hall. Four years later, Philadelphians organized one of America's first historic preservation efforts and saved the hall as a museum.

During this same period, the survival of the Liberty Bell was also in doubt. A proposal in 1816 to melt the bell down nearly succeeded. The protests of Philadelphians stopped that plan, and over the next century, Americans transformed the Liberty Bell from a neglected colonial relic to a world-famous icon of freedom.

The first reference to Philadelphia's State House Bell as the Liberty Bell was in an 1839 pamphlet by William Lloyd Garrison promoting the abolition of slavery. It is ironic that as the reputation of the bell grew in the antebellum period, its large and distinctive crack, caused by excessive ringing and unsuccessful repair work, also grew and silenced it forever in 1846. Following the Civil War, devotion to the Liberty Bell increased to a quasi-religious obsession. Without a state church, Americans adopted the Liberty Bell as a sacred relic. It was the major attraction at the 1876 Centennial Exposition in Philadelphia. Between 1885 and 1915, the Liberty Bell journeyed to seven fairs and expositions throughout the country.

The last and most spectacular exhibit of the bell took place at the 1915 Panama-Pacific International Exposition in San Francisco. The Liberty Bell Train carrying the bell left Philadelphia on July 5, 1915, for a 10,000-mile, five-month journey through 30 states, with stops in 173 cities and towns, where millions of people lined up to see, touch, photograph, and even kiss the bell. At the exposition itself, the bell attracted around two million people, easily the fair's most popular exhibit.

By the mid-twentieth century, the Liberty Bell and Independence Hall were the leading tourist attractions in Philadelphia. The establishment of Independence National Historical Park in the 1950s gave the National Park Service responsibility for preservation and interpretation. Public funding and private support from the Pew Charitable Trusts and other philanthropic organizations have achieved impressive results.

The recent history of Independence Park has not been without conflict or controversy. During the construction of a new Liberty Bell pavilion in 1998, archaeologists found extensive evidence of the house George Washington lived in during his presidency, including artifacts related to slaves who worked as household servants. Political and academic leaders protested that a shrine to liberty was incomplete and dishonest without recognizing the existence of slavery in eighteenth-century Philadelphia. Today, an outdoor exhibit adjacent to the pavilion tells the story of Washington's enslaved servants and the efforts of one of them—Horace—to secure his freedom.

Philadelphia's Benjamin Franklin himself has secured a permanent place in America's pantheon. A throng estimated at twenty thousand followed his funeral procession in 1790 to his gravesite in the Christ Church Burial Ground, and the nation observed a month of mourning. Within Independence Park, a new interactive museum has opened next to Franklin Court, a unique steel-framed structure designed by Robert Venturi and Denise Scott Brown. Along Benjamin Franklin Parkway, the Franklin Institute is home to the Benjamin Franklin National Memorial, featuring an enormous statue by James Earle Fraser (1911). Surely, there is little risk that this great American will be forgotten.

WEBSITES

Independence National Historical Park, www.nps.gov/inde
Franklin Court, www.nps.gov/inde/fragments-of-franklin-court.htm
Benjamin Franklin National Memorial, www.nps.gov/inde/benjamin
    -franklin-national-memorial.htm
American Philosophical Society, www.amphilsoc.org

NEARBY PLACES

Betsy Ross House, www.historicphiladelphia.org/betsy-ross-house
    /what-to-see

Christ Church Burial Ground, www.christchurchphila.org/historic
    -christ-church/burial-ground/59

Carpenters' Hall, www.ushistory.org/carpentershall

Edgar Allan Poe National Historic Site, www.nps.gov/edal

10

VIRGINIA PENINSULA
YORKTOWN, VIRGINIA

The Yorktown Victory Monument

When King George III of England heard that George Washington planned to resign as commander of the American army in 1783, he said, "If he does that, he will be the greatest man in the world." Given that Washington had fought England for six years and sent five of her best generals home in defeat, this was high praise indeed.

Washington's triumph at Yorktown, Virginia, on October 19, 1781, decisively ended America's War for Independence. Victory came after a three-year British campaign in the southern colonies of Georgia, the Carolinas, and Virginia, where General George Clinton hoped to attract Loyalists who did not support independence. In December 1778, the British captured Savannah, and in June 1780, Charleston fell after a six-week siege. General Clinton returned to his base in New York and left the southern command to General Charles Cornwallis, who directed his army into the Carolina backcountry in the fall of 1780. Instead of attracting Loyalists to their side, the British army sparked strong resistance from American patriots in crucial battles at Kings Mountain and Cowpens.

The British were victorious at Guilford Courthouse (near present-day Greensboro, North Carolina) on March 15, 1781, but nearly a quarter of their force were killed or wounded, causing a British politician to observe, "Another such victory would ruin the British army." In May 1781, Cornwallis marched back to the coast, first to Wilmington, North Carolina, and then to Yorktown, a seaport strategically located between the York and James Rivers on the Virginia Peninsula. There he established a naval base and built a series of small earthworks, redoubts, to secure his position. At his command were nineteen ships and 8,500 soldiers.

This stronghold did not last long. George Washington invited France, an American ally since 1778, to join in attacking Cornwallis. On September 5, a fleet of French warships battled the British navy, forcing them to retreat to New York and leaving Cornwallis without safe passage to the sea. In late September, 9,000 American troops under Washington's command and a force of 8,000 French soldiers led by Comte du Rochambeau began a siege of Yorktown. Their constant barrage of artillery fire wore down the British defenses. By mid-October, the American and French forces were within four hundred yards of the British defenses and able to attack at will. On October 17, 1781, a British drummer boy mounted a redoubt and tapped out a call for surrender. Two days later, the entire British army laid down their swords while, according to some accounts, their band played "The World Turned Upside Down." Although the British still maintained 26,000 troops in America, a new government in London decided to end the conflict. On September 3, 1783, the Treaty of Paris granted recognition to the United States of America. The American victory was a vindication of Washington's extraordinary leadership, which he demonstrated throughout the war and later as America's first president. After his death in 1799, Henry Lee, a Revolutionary War comrade, eulogized him as "first in war, first in peace, and first in the hearts of his countrymen."

Significant historic landmarks on the Virginia Peninsula represent four centuries of American history. Several Civil War sites are in the southern portion of the peninsula. Fort Monroe, fifteen miles south of Yorktown, is the nation's largest stone fort. In 1861, its commander, Union general Benjamin Butler, refused to return fugitive slaves, claiming they were "contraband" of war. Within a few months, almost a thousand fugitive slaves had established a small colony outside the walls of the fort. In spring 1862, Fort Monroe was the staging site for a Union offensive known as the Peninsula Campaign, when General George McClellan led 100,000 troops from the fort through Yorktown and Williamsburg to within a few miles of Richmond, capital of the Confederacy.

McClellan's forces were able to land at Fort Monroe after the historic

Battle of the Ironclads between the USS *Monitor* and the USS *Merrimack* on March 9, 1862. The *Monitor* neutralized the Confederate navy and sailed up the James River, providing support for McClellan's army. At Newport News, fourteen miles from Fort Monroe, the Mariners' Museum displays artifacts from the *Monitor*, including its engine and turret, an innovation that revolutionized battleship design. The museum has a strong collection, exhibiting artifacts related to the area's important maritime and naval history.

Colonial history on the Virginia Peninsula is represented at Jamestown, the site of the first permanent English settlement in North America in 1607, twenty miles west of Yorktown. Historical documentation and pioneering archaeological research has produced dramatic insight into the beginnings of representative government, the challenges of daily life, relations with American Indians, and the origins of slavery in America.

Another landmark, Colonial Williamsburg, thirteen miles west of Yorktown, is a three-hundred-acre historic park that tells the story of Virginia's eighteenth-century capital. By the 1920s, Williamsburg was a town in decline with the exception of the beautiful campus of the College of William & Mary. A local Episcopal minister, the Reverend W. A. R. Goodwin, campaigned to restore the former capital to its eighteenth-century appearance. He enlisted the support of John D. Rockefeller Jr., and their efforts preserved more than eighty colonial buildings. When Colonial Williamsburg opened to the public in 1934, it was a milestone in America's historic preservation movement, sparking an increase in historic house museums and the practice of living history. The Colonial Williamsburg style also influenced the architecture of twentieth-century houses and towns. Most important, the Colonial Williamsburg Foundation, with its support for scholarship and innovative programming, has led the effort to teach American history and critically examine the founding principles and challenges of self-government.

Shortly after Williamsburg opened to the public, construction began on the Colonial Parkway, a twenty-three-mile scenic road that links Yorktown, Williamsburg, and Jamestown. Completed in 1957, it is itself a historic landmark, the first road built and managed by the National Park Service. By unifying the three colonial sites, removing commercial intrusions, and integrating natural and cultural resources, the parkway promoted preservation and tourism. It continues to serve today as the gateway to the story of building, defending, and preserving American democracy.

WEBSITES

Mariners' Museum and Park, www.marinersmuseum.org
Colonial National Historical Park, www.nps.gov/colo
Colonial Williamsburg Foundation, www.colonialwilliamsburg.com
Historic Jamestown, www.historicjamestown.org

NEARBY PLACES

Virginia Historical Society, www.vahistorical.org
Richmond History, www.visitrichmondva.com
Virginia Living Museum, www.thevlm.org
Fort Monroe National Monument, www.nps.gov/fomr

11

MONTICELLO
CHARLOTTESVILLE, VIRGINIA

Monticello

Monticello, Thomas Jefferson's extraordinary Virginia home, has a history and personality as complex as the man who built it. Jefferson's first design reflected his admiration for the architectural principles of Andrea Palladio, a sixteenth-century Italian architect and writer. Palladio's *I quattro libri dell'architettura* (*The Four Books of Architecture*), published in 1570, was the most influential architectural text of the Renaissance. He emphasized classical features such as columns and porticos and, above all, a sense of balance and proportion. He also encouraged locating buildings in settings that symbolized their power and significance. Jefferson first learned of these ideas through books written by James Gibbs, an eighteenth-century English architect.

Jefferson began building Monticello (Italian for "little mountain") in 1769, following Palladio's principles. His design closely resembled the Villa Cornaro (1552) in Venice, which had a three-part façade with a double portico in the center supported by Corinthian columns and a hipped roof on each wing. After Jefferson served as minister to France in the 1780s, he added elements of French neoclassicism, most notably a dome, the first of its kind in America, which gives the house its distinctive appearance today. Throughout his life, he continued to alter the design of the house and added new features such as a one-thousand-foot-long terraced vegetable garden that blended varieties from France, England, Spain, the Mediterranean, and elsewhere. Jefferson considered vegetables "my principal diet" and included produce from European, American Indian, African, and Creole traditions.

Although Jefferson spent more than forty years in public life, he preferred to think of himself as a private man, a farmer, a man of science dedicated to education and liberal thought. His tombstone in the cemetery at Monticello reads:

> *Here was buried*
> *Thomas Jefferson*
> *Author of the*
> *Declaration of American Independence*
> *Of the*
> *Statute of Virginia*
> *for Religious Freedom*
> *And Father of the*
> *University of Virginia*

Curiously, there is no reference to his public service as governor of Virginia, minister to France, U.S. secretary of state, or vice president of the United States. Nor is there any mention that he served two terms, from 1801 to 1809, as the third president of the United States, and that he doubled the nation's size with the Louisiana Purchase in 1803.

Monticello was a symbol of architectural independence when America was waging its war for political independence and establishing a new experiment in self-government. Through the lens of the twenty-first century, we recognize the new nation's central contradiction: the enslavement of 680,000 men, women, and children. Nowhere was this contradiction more evident than at Monticello, where Jefferson used slave labor to build and maintain his home and plantation. During Jefferson's lifetime as many as 600 African slaves lived at Monticello and his other plantations, and in any given year, 130 slaves worked in construction, farming and gardening, and household work. Monticello's Mulberry Row was the center of work and domestic life with more than thirty buildings housing a variety of enterprises and dwellings, including a profitable nail-making operation, established in 1794, where young boys aged ten to sixteen produced thousands of nails for sale to plantations in Jefferson's county and others nearby.

While Jefferson wrote about the moral evils of slavery and predicted that a civil war might one day divide the United States, he depended on slave labor to operate his plantations. He hired overseers to maintain control of the slave population and sold or gave away slaves to resolve debts or to provide dowries for his children. Most historians now believe that after his wife's death, Jefferson fathered six children with an enslaved servant, Sally Hemings (who was also his wife's half sister), four of whom—Eston, Beverly, Harriet, and Madison—lived to adulthood.

After Jefferson retired to Monticello in 1809, he completed the major construction at his estate and continued to pursue projects that reflected his astounding intellectual and scientific interests. The interior details in the house included innovations such as dumbwaiters, skylights, alcove beds, and triple-sash windows. He bought scientific instruments and continued lifelong hobbies as a collector of natural history artifacts, coins, and especially books. He once confessed to a friend, "I labor grievously under the malady of bibliomania." In 1815, after he had acquired more than 6,500 books and was overwhelmed by personal debts, he sold his book collection, including rare editions of Palladio's treatise on architecture, to the Library of Congress.

One collection he did not sell was six copies of the New Testament in English, French, Greek, and Latin that he saved for a special project. Even though he did not actively practice any religion, he was a student of theology. In 1817, he began to cut out passages that he believed reflected true accounts of the life and teachings of Jesus Christ. After three years of patiently pasting these passages on sheets of rag paper, he had the book bound, and he read daily from his customized version of the Bible.

Jefferson ranks as one of America's great architects not only for Monticello but also for landmarks such as Virginia's State Capitol in Richmond (1788); Poplar Forest, the small Palladian-style retreat he began building near Lynchburg in 1806; and the Rotunda and grounds at the University of Virginia (1825). After his death, Monticello survived largely through the efforts of Uriah Levy and his nephew, Jefferson Monroe Levy, who bought and preserved the house and surrounding land for nearly a century. In 1923, the Thomas Jefferson Memorial Foundation purchased the house and nearly 700 acres (later expanded to 2,200 acres) and opened the site to visitors. In 1987, UNESCO recognized the estate and the University of Virginia as a World Heritage Site. The foundation opened a new museum and education center in 2009, and continues to be an international leader in historic site interpretation and Jeffersonian scholarship.

Virginia's eighteenth-century architectural and political heritage is unsurpassed and includes important historic sites—George Washington's Mount Vernon, James Madison's Montpelier, James Monroe's Ash Lawn, Patrick Henry's Scotchtown and Red Hill, Richard Henry Lee's Stratford Hall, and George Mason's Gunston Hall. These homes collectively tell the story of the nation's founding generation as well as the everyday lives of people—white and black, free and enslaved—who created a new nation based on individual rights and self-government.

WEBSITES

Monticello, www.monticello.org

University of Virginia, www.virginia.edu

Poplar Forest, www.poplarforest.org

Virginia State Capitol, www.virginiacapitol.gov

Thomas Jefferson Exhibition at the Library of Congress, www.loc.gov
/exhibits/jefferson

NEARBY PLACES

Mount Vernon, www.mountvernon.org

Montpelier, www.montpelier.org

Ash Lawn-Highland, www.ashlawnhighland.org

Gunston Hall, www.gunstonhall.org

Scotchtown, www.preservationvirginia.org/visit/historic-properties
/patrick-henrys-scotchtown

Red Hill, www.redhill.org

Stratford Hall, www.stratfordhall.org

12

THE PRESIDIO AT THE GOLDEN GATE

SAN FRANCISCO, CALIFORNIA

Fort Point at the Golden Gate

When U.S. Army captain John Charles Frémont saw the entrance to San Francisco Bay in 1846, he recognized the significance of the site. "To this gate," he wrote, "I gave the name 'Chrysophylae'—'Golden Gate' in Greek—for the same reasons that the harbor of Byzantium was called 'Chysoceras,' or 'Golden Horn.'" Frémont's prophecy came true. The bay became the gateway to a major port, a magnificent city, and the centerpiece of America's western and Pacific empire. Extraordinary natural beauty and remarkable history combine here to define our national experience. A trip through the Presidio is a trip not only through military history but also through architectural history, with some four hundred historically significant structures ranging from Spanish Mission style at Fort Scott to Civil War cottages on Funston Avenue, late nineteenth-century brick officers' barracks on the Main Post, and Georgian Revival, Art Deco, and International-style structures.

Before the Americans occupied this site, the Spanish recognized its strategic importance. Between 1769 and 1782, Spanish soldiers established four presidios—fortified garrisons—along the coast of Alta ("upper," or northern) California. Located in San Diego, Santa Barbara, Monterey, and San Francisco, they protected the northern boundary of Spain's colonial empire in America from English, French, and Russian rivals. The Presidio at San Francisco was the northernmost Spanish fort, established in 1776 by Lieutenant Colonel Juan Bautista de Anza, who led nearly three hundred men, women, and children on an epic 1,375-mile, six-month journey that began in Sonora, Mexico. The four presidios supported twenty-four missions and a few small villages of colonists. Fifty years of Spanish occupation had tragic consequences for American

Indians, including the Ohlone people, who had occupied these lands for centuries. Their numbers declined dramatically through military conflicts and, as in most North American colonies, infectious diseases such as smallpox and measles.

After winning independence in 1821, Mexico maintained the California presidios but in the 1830s gave priority to securing its eastern border with the Republic of Texas. When the United States defeated Mexico in 1848, it established a permanent military base at the Presidio to guard the entrance to the bay and its potentially valuable harbor. Over the next century, the Presidio was the heart of coastal defense in the West. It also served a dual role as a base for continental expansion during the Indian Wars of the 1870s and 1880s, and as a command post for America's emergence as an imperial power during the Spanish-American War (1898) and the conflict in the Philippines (1901–1904). As the Presidio grew in its responsibilities, the Army created five commands: Main Post, Fort Point, Letterman Hospital, Fort Winfield Scott, and Crissy Air Field, which included a Coast Guard lifesaving station. Alcatraz, later the site of the infamous federal prison, and Angel Island, an immigration processing center, were also managed from the Presidio. In World War II, the Army established the Presidio as headquarters for coastal defense, combat operations in the Aleutian Islands, and military intelligence provided by Japanese American soldiers. From his Presidio office, General John L. DeWitt implemented Executive Order 9066, which led to the forced internment of 120,000 Japanese Americans.

Today, the Presidio contains a rich variety of military engineering landmarks, including Fort Point (1861) with brick walls seven to twelve feet thick and three tiers of vaulted rooms for cannon. After the Civil War, the Army constructed earthworks, built concrete batteries, and established the West Coast's first aviation field, during World War I. In World War II, minefields, antiaircraft guns, and an antisubmarine net protected the harbor from attack. During the Cold War, a Nike missile site, one of twelve installed in the San Francisco Bay area in the 1950s, provided the last example of the Presidio's stunning variety of weaponry.

Although the Army removed or scrapped nearly all the guns, missiles, and other weapons from the Presidio, a visitor can see the evidence of military history everywhere. Fort Point survives, as do fifteen batteries that once housed three generations of artillery.

One of the Presidio's most remarkable and surprising legacies is the three-hundred-acre forest created in the late nineteenth century. Following a plan drafted by Major William A. Jones in 1883, the Army planted thousands of trees—eucalyptus, pine, and cypress. The beautification project is a signature feature of the park, even though scientists today recognize that some varieties were incompatible with the Presidio's unique microclimate and ecology. Well-marked trails provide easily accessible walks or jogs through forests and meadows with unsurpassed views of San Francisco Bay, the Golden Gate Bridge, and the hills of Marin County.

Dramatic events outside the Presidio's borders also shaped its history. After San Francisco's 1906 earthquake and fire, the Army created four relief camps, including a separate camp for Chinese residents. In 1915, the Panama-Pacific International Exposition used post sites for foreign pavilions, livestock exhibitions, and an automobile racetrack. The construction of the Golden Gate Bridge in 1937 required access roads that divided the base, but this structure quickly became a distinctive part of the landscape, a landmark recognized around the world.

The bridge was one of many factors that contributed to rapid growth in the Bay Area. By 1960 industrial pollution and encroachments along the shoreline had reduced the size of the bay by a third. In response, three women—Kay Kerr, Sylvia McLaughlin, and Esther Gulick—organized a grassroots conservation movement, one of the nation's first, in 1961. Their organization, Save San Francisco Bay Association, successfully lobbied to create the Bay Conservation and Development Commission in 1965. Another milestone in protecting the resources of the region was the establishment of the Golden Gate National Recreation Area (GGNRA) in 1972, a bipartisan effort led by Congressman Phil Burton.

The Presidio reflects and continues San Francisco's history of community activism on behalf of the environment. In 1996, Congress created the Presidio Trust. In partnership with the National Park Service, it manages 1,500 acres within the Golden Gate National Recreation Area. The trust has fulfilled its government mandate to become financially self-sufficient, while balancing competing claims of development, preservation, and commemoration. The trust constructed twenty-four miles of trails, initiated an ambitious reforestation program, and preserved three hundred buildings. These include the former Officers' Club, containing remnants of the Spanish Presidio, now transformed into a center for historical exhibitions, cultural programs, and archaeological research. Today, the Presidio is a vibrant public space where people live, work, and play.

WEBSITES
The Presidio, www.presidio.gov
Presidio of San Francisco, www.nps.gov/prsf
San Francisco National Cemetery, www.nps.gov/prsf/historyculture
    /san-francisco-national-cemetery.htm

NEARBY PLACES
Golden Gate Bridge, www.goldengatebridge.org
Alcatraz Island, www.nps.gov/alca
Cable Car Museum, www.cablecarmuseum.org
The Walt Disney Family Museum, www.waltdisney.org
Museum of the African Diaspora, www.moadsf.org

13

WHITE DOVE OF THE DESERT

TUCSON, ARIZONA

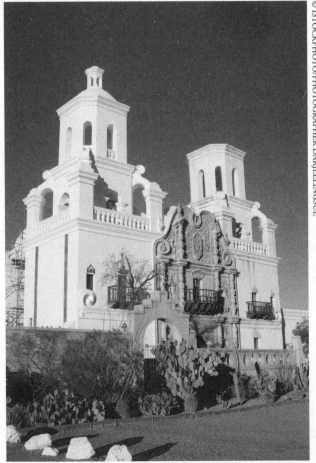

Mission San Xavier

Among the last churches built by the Spanish in North America is perhaps the most beautiful. Mission San Xavier del Bac, known as the "White Dove of the Desert," stands in peaceful isolation in the Sonoran Desert, ten miles south of Tucson. The oldest European structure in Arizona, it is considered by many to be the finest example of Spanish Colonial architecture in the United States.

While Spanish conquistadors aggressively exploited the riches of South and Central America in the sixteenth century, the absence of mineral wealth to the north led to a long period of benign neglect. When England, France, and Russia expanded their colonial interests in North America in the seventeenth and eighteenth centuries, Spain's colonial rulers secured their borders by building presidios and by encouraging various Catholic orders—Dominican, Franciscan, and Jesuit—to pacify and convert the native Indians. Some tribes, such as the Apaches, resisted the conversion campaigns. In other locations, Indian interest in Christianity declined during epidemics caused by contact with Europeans.

The seminomadic Tohono O'odham people of the Sonoran Desert eventually played a significant role in building Mission San Xavier. The Spanish called them Pima and referred to their land as Pimería Alta in what is now Sonora, Mexico, and southern Arizona, a vast desert more than 100,000 square miles, and the hottest in North America. In 1692, Jesuit priest Father Eusebio Francisco Kino visited the Tohono O'odham village of Wa:k (called Bac by the Jesuits) and founded the Mission San Xavier del Bac. Born in Italy and educated in Germany as a mathematician, cartographer, and astronomer, Kino was also interested in ranching and agricultural science. Arriving in Mexico in 1681, he crisscrossed the

Southwest, discovering a land route to Baja California and producing the first maps of that region and the Pimería Alta. He founded twenty-four missions, introduced cattle ranching and wheat farming to the Tohono O'odham, and earned their trust through his criticism of the Spanish government's use of Indian slave labor in mining and farming. Father Kino died in 1711, before construction began on the church he planned to build at Bac. His statue stands in National Statuary Hall of the U.S. Capitol.

By the 1750s, Spanish settlement had spread along the Santa Cruz River valley, leading to clashes with the natives. The Pima Revolt of 1751 resulted in the deaths of more than a hundred Spanish settlers. In response, the Spanish built new presidios, including one at Tubac. They also turned against the Jesuits, an independent international order based in Rome, whom they blamed for encouraging the natives' revolt. This conflict led to the Jesuits' expulsion from New Spain in 1767. The next year, the Franciscan order took over San Xavier and other Jesuit missions in Pimería Alta, and in 1776, Father Juan Bautista Velderrain, resident priest at Mission San Xavier, planned a new church. Borrowing 7,000 pesos from a Spanish rancher, he engaged a Sonoran architect, Ignatio Gaona, and hired Tohono O'odham natives as laborers. Work began in 1783 and progressed slowly as funding permitted. Gaona's design, blending Baroque, Moorish, and Byzantine styles, is unusual for Spanish missions. The church is made of clay bricks and stone set in lime mortar and covered with lime plaster, and the church complex includes a mortuary chapel, a convent, dormitory, patio, and garden.

Two bell towers flank a center section decorated in Baroque style, with Franciscan cord and seashells, the symbol of pilgrimage, utilized as motifs throughout. The mission's interior is breathtaking. Carved wooden statues of the Virgin Mary and Saint Francis along with statues of other saints and American Indians, several dressed in hand-sewn clothing, fill the sanctuary. Large paintings on plaster and wood carvings are in the choir loft and main chamber. The sculptures were probably made in Querétaro, Mexico, in guild workshops, transported north on donkeys. The designer of this amazing scene is not known, but Native craftsmen deserve much credit for executing a complex and intricate plan. Work continued for more than a decade, but with costs rising well beyond the original budget, construction stopped in 1797 with one tower and some interior painting unfinished.

When Mexico gained its independence from Spain in 1821, the new republic tried to control the Franciscan missions. The priest at San Xavier, Father Rafael Diaz, protested this policy and resigned in 1828. After the Gadsden Purchase of 1853 made southern Arizona a part of the United States, the mission regained its connection with the Catholic Church, becoming part of the Santa Fe Diocese in 1859. The San Xavier Reservation, created for the Tohono O'odham people in 1874, included the mission, which still serves the reservation today.

Preservation of Mission San Xavier has been a major concern. In the twentieth century, the diocese launched an initiative to repair damage caused by an 1887 earthquake and to renovate the church complex. Since 1978, a nonprofit group, Patronato San Xavier, has sponsored the conservation of the art and architecture of this National Historic Landmark. The chapel is open free of charge every day except during church events.

Within sixty miles south of Tucson are major historic sites associated with Spanish colonial history. Tumacácori Mission, originally founded by Father Kino and partially completed by Franciscans in the early nineteenth century, is part of a national historic park. Nearby, Tubac Presidio State Historic Park preserves the ruins of the Spanish fort built after the Pima Revolt of 1751. The courthouse at Nogales, located at the Mexican border, houses an exhibit on the historic Juan Bautista de Anza expedition of 1775–76, now a National Historic Trail, which stopped at Mission San Xavier en route to founding San Francisco. About a half hour's drive west of Tucson is the Arizona-Sonora Desert Museum. With unique outdoor interactive experiences, this museum provides an understanding of the natural resources that shaped the history of this region and the need to preserve them.

WEBSITES

Mission San Xavier del Bac, www.sanxaviermission.org

Arizona-Sonora Desert Museum, www.desertmuseum.org

Tohono O'odham Nation, www.tonation-nsn.gov

NEARBY PLACES

Tubac Presidio State Historic Park, www.azstateparks.com/Parks
    /TUPR/index.html

Arizona Historical Society, www.arizonahistoricalsociety.org

St. Augustine Cathedral, www.staugustinecathedral.org

Titan Missile Museum, www.titanmissilemuseum.org

14

SLATER MILL

PAWTUCKET, RHODE ISLAND

Slater Mill

It is a myth that Samuel Slater was a poor, uneducated immigrant worker from England who memorized the textile manufacturing process and single-handedly created America's first successful textile mill. In fact, Slater was an experienced, knowledgeable management trainee and his success depended on capital from entrepreneurs and on the labor of men, women, and children in his adopted home of Pawtucket, Rhode Island.

Slater was born in 1768 in the central England county of Derbyshire, the same year and the same place that Richard Arkwright, a pioneer of the industrial revolution, developed new machinery for preparing and spinning cotton into yarn. Arkwright's patented machinery was a turning point in industrial history. What had once required hundreds of hours by dozens of laborers now could be accomplished by machinery operated by just a few workers, usually young boys and girls.

Samuel Slater was not one of those children tending machinery. His father was a prosperous real estate investor who wanted his son to learn about the new textile machinery that was changing England's industrial landscape. In 1782, he hired his son to apprentice with Richard Arkwright's partner, Jedidiah Strutt. Samuel concentrated on bookkeeping, mill management, and mechanical operations.

The manufacturing principles Slater learned represented the core elements of the industrial revolution: harnessing power to move machinery, keeping machinery in continuous motion, and positioning machines efficiently in relation to each other. In the eighteenth century, manufacturers made use of abundant waterpower along England's rivers and streams. Waterwheels powered an intricate system of gears, shafts, pulleys, and belts that kept a mill's carding, drawing, and spinning machinery in motion day and night. Carding involved running cotton fibers through machines with wire brushes that combed and straightened the fiber into a thick strand called a sliver. The sliver was transferred to drawing machines that stretched the fiber into longer and thinner strands. Finally, the strands of cotton were fed to spinning machines that, like a spinning wheel, twisted and turned the fiber tightly into uniform strands. Success in this enterprise depended on having the proper number of machines for each step to maintain a continuous flow of production.

With this fundamental knowledge of power technology, textile machinery, and business management, Slater completed his apprenticeship in 1789 and, at the age of twenty-one, immigrated to America, seeking greater opportunity. Because the English government did not allow either the export of machinery designs or the emigration of skilled mechanics, Slater disguised himself as a poor farmworker and boarded a ship for New York. There he heard that merchants in Rhode Island were trying to develop textile manufacturing. Moses Brown, a Quaker businessman, led this effort. He bought carding and spinning machinery and set up operations in Pawtucket, a shipbuilding town with an ideal site for water-powered industry at the falls of the Blackstone River.

Brown recruited Slater to organize and operate his Pawtucket factory. By 1793, Slater succeeded in developing a mill that produced yarn for weaving and knitting. The Old Slater Mill, the first successful cotton mill in America, was a simple frame building less than 1,500 square feet that looked like the English mills Slater knew as an apprentice. Five years later, he built a more substantial structure, known as the White Mill, on the eastern bank of the Blackstone. In this new venture, Slater integrated his technical knowledge with the management principles he had learned in Derbyshire. By the age of thirty, he had earned recognition as a pioneer in the industrial revolution.

Slater and other textile manufacturers benefited from a significant technological breakthrough—Eli Whitney's cotton gin, invented in 1793, which quickly removed seeds from cotton fibers and turned cotton cultivation into a profitable business. A greater supply of cotton from Southern plantations along with abundant waterpower and cheap labor allowed textile manufacturing to spread throughout New England. By 1840, the largest textile center was in Lowell, Massachusetts, with thirty-one mills operating along a complex network of power canals and employing around eight thousand workers, mostly women from nearby farms.

Later, in the nineteenth and early twentieth centuries, the mills needed more workers and attracted immigrants from Canada, Ireland, Italy, and Eastern Europe. These new recruits supported unions that organized to bargain on their behalf and to strike, if necessary, for higher wages and better working conditions. The most celebrated labor action was the Bread and Roses strike of 1912 in Lawrence, Massachusetts, when thirty thousand workers staged a nine-week strike that attracted national attention and resulted in significant reforms.

After World War I, the center of America's textile industry shifted to the South, where manufacturers could build new mills and expand existing facilities at lower cost using cheap hydroelectric power and nonunion labor. In North Carolina, for example, the number of mills increased from 293 in 1914 to 343 in 1921. During that same period, the number of workers grew by 25 percent and the value of all textile production went from $90 million to $190 million. Despite long periods of labor peace, major conflicts took place in Gastonia and Marion in 1929 and again in 1934, when more than four hundred thousand workers nationwide staged a three-week general strike, the largest in U.S. history.

In the twenty-first century, textile production is not a major American industry. However, several important initiatives have preserved the public memory of its formative years. At the small but most impressive Slater Mill complex, visitors can tour Old Slater Mill with displays about textile manufacturing history. Next door, the 1810 Wilkinson Mill machine shop exhibits a spectacular demonstration of waterpower that includes a wooden wheel and original line shaft, belts, and pulleys that still drive drills, lathes, and other machines.

Slater Mill is part of the Blackstone River Valley National Heritage

Corridor, a National Park Service program designed to encourage the preservation of historic places and to promote tourism. The corridor stretches from Worcester, Massachusetts, to Providence, Rhode Island. Many regions have strong claims on contributing to America's industrial heritage; however, one of the best starting points is in Pawtucket along the Blackstone River, thanks to the ingenuity and skill of Samuel Slater.

WEBSITES
Slater Mill, www.slatermill.org
Blackstone River Valley National Heritage Corridor, www.nps.gov/blac

NEARBY PLACES
Rhode Island Historical Society, www.rihs.org
Roger Williams National Memorial, www.nps.gov/rowi
Providence Athenaeum, www.providenceathenaeum.org
Governor Stephen Hopkins House, www.visitrhodeisland.com/what
    -to-see/mansions-and-historic-homes/512/governor-stephen
    -hopkins-house

15

VILLAGE GREEN

HUDSON, OHIO

Hudson Clock Tower

In 1800, thirty Connecticut residents migrated to a new settlement in a section of northeastern Ohio known as the Western Reserve. The previous year, David Hudson and a group of surveyors had laid out the town that would bear his name. He was one of thirty-five shareholders in the Connecticut Land Company who had purchased more than three million acres of land at forty cents an acre from the state of Connecticut in 1795, thereby ending the state's long-standing claim to land that extended west to the Pacific Ocean. The land company encouraged settlement by selling tracts to Connecticut developers who brought with them traditions of town planning, religious faith, antislavery politics, and support for education. Hudson has retained this New England heritage anchored by a ten-acre village green and scores of well-preserved homes, churches, businesses, and public buildings from the nineteenth and early twentieth centuries.

Within ten years after its founding, around two hundred people lived in Hudson. Those first families included Owen Brown, his wife, Ruth, their daughter, and three sons. The oldest boy, John, was five when the family left Torrington, Connecticut, and made a five-hundred-mile, forty-eight-day journey along the southern tier of New York, south through Pittsburgh, and across the Allegheny River to the Mahoning Indian trail that led to the Western Reserve. Owen Brown built a log cabin on the north side of the village green and eventually owned a small farm and tannery. A leader in education, he was an incorporator of Western Reserve College (1826), sometimes referred to as the Yale of the West, and a trustee of Oberlin Collegiate Institute (1833) in nearby Elyria, now Oberlin College in Oberlin, Ohio.

Both schools established reputations for academic excellence and for promoting the abolitionist movement that grew in Ohio and other Northern states in the 1830s and 1840s. Hudson was one of the earliest centers of the Underground Railroad, with at least ten stations in operation, including one at Owen Brown's home. Thousands of enslaved men, women, and children made the perilous journey along the Ohio River, called the River Jordan by fugitives, and its tributaries to Lake Erie and on to Canada, referred to as "the Promised Land."

John Brown spent his youth in Hudson, absorbing his father's strict Calvinist faith and his passionate opposition to slavery. He left Hudson in 1820 to start a utopian community in Pennsylvania but returned in 1825 to establish a tannery north of town. A converted hayloft in his barn became an Underground Railroad station. In 1837, in reaction to the murder of an Illinois abolitionist editor, Brown stood up in Hudson's Congregational Church and declared, "Here, before God, in the presence of these witnesses, from this time, I consecrate my life to the destruction of slavery."

In the 1850s, Brown grew more militant in his opposition to slavery. In 1855, he joined his sons and other pioneers in Kansas to promote that territory as a free state and engaged in several violent clashes with proslavery forces, which caused the state to become known as "Bleeding Kansas." In May 1856 he organized the defense of Lawrence, and a few weeks later, led a brutal attack in Pottawatomie that killed five proslavery men. Before the conflict ended in 1859, fifty-six men on both sides had died. Brown was now a celebrated and notorious abolitionist. He journeyed through the Northern states, including a stop in Hudson, to raise money and attract supporters for his audacious and dramatic attack on the federal arsenal in Harpers Ferry, Virginia, on October 16, 1859. Brown's hope that the raid would inspire a national liberation movement did not materialize; he was captured and executed on December 2. Most historians agree that the Harpers Ferry raid was a leading cause of the Civil War.

During the antebellum decades, Hudson prospered as a commercial center with the completion of the Ohio and Erie Canal in 1825 and the arrival of the Cleveland and Pittsburgh Railroad, completed in 1851. However, the financial panic of 1857 led to a gradual decline for the rest of the nineteenth century. Western Reserve College (now Case Western Reserve University), faced with shrinking enrollment, relocated to Cleveland in 1882. A major fire in 1892 destroyed much of the central business district and many residents left town for opportunities in larger cities.

One exception to this exodus was James Ellsworth, a Hudson native who left in 1869 and earned an enormous fortune in coal mining and banking. He returned in 1907 and found Hudson in a deplorable state. He made a personal commitment to create a "model town" with paved streets, new utilities, and other public improvements. As a symbol of renewal, Ellsworth built a clock tower on the village green in 1912. Designed by F. Howard Clockworks of Boston, it remains the centerpiece of a town that prides itself on its rich history, well-preserved architecture, and a lively cultural life.

Ellsworth was an early supporter of the Hudson Library and Historical Society, founded by Caroline Baldwin Babcock, which continues today as a valuable research institution and an advocate for preserving the town's heritage. The society sponsors programs on local history and guided walking tours on various themes. The tour on the abolitionist movement includes sites where John Brown harbored fugitive slaves, where he first spoke publicly against slavery, and where he addressed a crowd in the summer of 1859 prior to his final battle in Harpers Ferry.

Hudson has a well-deserved reputation for historic preservation. Two large historic districts comprise more than five hundred buildings that reflect every style and period from the earliest settlement. Highlights include the Loomis Observatory (1838), the oldest astronomical observatory in the United States, other buildings associated with Case Western Reserve University, and a residential district near downtown with dozens of examples of Greek Revival and Victorian architecture. The town retains its New England plan organized around the village green, the setting for festivals, farmer's markets, and holiday events. It provides an enduring connection to small-town values, ideals, and traditions that shaped American democracy.

WEBSITES
Hudson Library and Historical Society, www.hudsonlibrary.org

NEARBY PLACES
Loomis Observatory, www.observatoriesofohio.org/loomis-observatory
Stan Hywet Hall & Gardens, www.stanhywet.org
Western Reserve Historical Society, www.wrhs.org
Cuyahoga Valley National Park, www.nps.gov/cuva

16

TWO UTOPIAS
NEW HARMONY, INDIANA

New Harmony Labyrinth

Communal societies played a small but influential role in American history. Although Americans chose capitalism as their economic model, the idea of communities based on collective ownership briefly offered an alternative to a system driven by markets, profits, and private property.

From 1814 to 1827, New Harmony, Indiana, was the site of two communal societies—one a great success, the other a great failure—that shared a common vision. Both depended on charismatic leadership that promoted communal ownership of property; self-sufficient economies based on agriculture, manufacturing, and crafts; and a rich cultural life featuring music, education, and science. Most important, both promised happiness for individual members through collective efforts.

From the earliest colonial settlements, Americans promoted the ideal of a social compact based on cooperation and mutual support. John Winthrop's sermon to his fellow Puritans as they sailed to Massachusetts in 1630 urged them to create "a model of Christian Charity" that the world would recognize "as a city on a hill." In 1681, William Penn founded Pennsylvania as "A Holy Experiment," expanding the meaning of a model community by ensuring religious freedom. Pennsylvania became a refuge for various groups, first attracting Penn's Quaker associates, then Mennonites, Amish, Schwenkfelders, Moravians, Seventh-Day Baptists, and the Harmonists, followers of George Rapp, a Lutheran minister from Württemberg, Germany.

Father Rapp was a Pietist who preached a more personal form of Christianity. By the 1780s, he had attracted a large congregation but also opposition from local church and government officials. In 1803, he led five hundred followers to America and searched for the best site for his congregation, even consulting with President Thomas Jefferson. He purchased land in western Pennsylvania, where he and his congregants established the Harmony Society, giving up their possessions in exchange for food, clothing, shelter, education, and religious instruction. They were Millennialists, believing that a thousand-year reign of Christ was imminent and they must live on earth as they would in heaven. They named their settlement Harmony based on their commitment to living in peace as individuals, with their neighbors, and with God.

The Harmonists enjoyed a good life in Pennsylvania sustained by farming and a highly profitable textile industry. During their decade in Harmony, Father Rapp and his successors practiced celibacy. Members agreed to forgo sexual relations and new members agreed to live in households segregated by sex. The society remained a celibate association for a century until its dissolution in 1905. This practice, as well as their commitments to pacifism and the abolition of slavery, created tensions with their neighbors.

By 1814, the society decided to move to a place where they could enjoy greater freedom. They purchased twenty thousand acres along the Wabash River in Indiana, five hundred miles west of their home, and built New Harmony. They constructed 180 buildings—houses, dormitories, a distillery and tavern, an enormous brick and stone granary, two churches, and steam-powered cotton and woolen mills. They traded with local farmers and nearby Shaker communities. Although they prospered in this wilderness setting, they realized they were too far from urban markets and found the hot summers along the Wabash intolerable. In January 1825 they sold New Harmony, moved back to Pennsylvania, and built a new town north of Pittsburgh called Economy. For several decades, even after Father Rapp's death in 1847, they enjoyed extraordinary prosperity, becoming one of the most successful communal groups in American history.

New Harmony's buyer was Robert Owen, a wealthy British industrialist and advocate of nonreligious cooperative communities. In the early nineteenth century, he transformed a textile mill community in

New Lanark, Scotland, into a model of progressive reform by improving working and living conditions for mill workers and providing better education for them and their children. Visitors from around the world flocked to New Lanark to see how Owen managed to operate profitably while offering a better life to his employees.

As Owen promoted reforms in labor law, he also devised a plan for self-governing cooperative communities. His ideas, however, met with resistance or indifference. He headed to America, purchased New Harmony for $200,000 (about $2.6 million in 2013), and set up a cooperative society in which members surrendered their personal property and agreed to work for the common good. In the first year, around a thousand people joined him in adapting the former Harmonist buildings for new purposes.

In November 1824, Owen visited Washington and received celebrity treatment. He met President Monroe, President-elect John Quincy Adams, and Andrew Jackson. He returned to Washington in the spring of 1825 and, at the invitation of House Speaker Henry Clay, he made two public speeches in the House of Representatives. Before leaving America, he met Thomas Jefferson at Monticello and James Madison at Montpelier. When he returned to England, he found that several Owenite communities had formed there based on his philosophy. He was at the height of his influence and prestige.

Life at New Harmony, however, was not harmonious. While residents enjoyed evening concerts, dances, and plays, they could not agree on the division of labor and would not agree to give up personal property. Dissident groups, one led by Owen's sons, threatened the unity of the association. Owen returned to America and his business partner, William Maclure, recruited some of the world's leading scientists and educators to join their community. Maclure, himself a famous geologist, commissioned a riverboat, *The Philanthropist*, which Owen nicknamed the "Boatload of Knowledge" in recognition of its illustrious passenger list. It carried the new members from Pittsburgh to New Harmony in January 1826. In response to his critics, Owen proposed a new constitution called the Community of Equality based on equal rights for men and women, communal ownership of property, freedom of speech, and "sincerity, kindness, courtesy, and order." None of Owen's reorganization efforts worked, however, and conflicts with Maclure created additional strain. By spring 1827, Owen recognized that his New Harmony experiment had failed.

While Owen's colony was short-lived, his legacy endured. In 1838, Maclure established the Working Men's Institute to provide education for manual laborers. One hundred sixty institutes opened in Indiana and Illinois; the last of these still operates in New Harmony. In the twentieth century, Jane Blaffer Owen, an oil heiress and philanthropist who married a Robert Owen descendant, joined the movement to restore and revive New Harmony and inspired a community revitalization. She commissioned Philip Johnson's Roofless Church (1960) and built a park dedicated to the theologian Paul Tillich. Additional support from the Lilly Foundation, the state of Indiana, and the University of Southern Indiana helped preserve two dozen Harmonist buildings. A new visitor center, the Atheneum, designed by Richard Meier, opened in 1979. On the edge of town, visitors can walk through a labyrinth reconstructed in 1939 near the original designed by Father George Rapp, a symbol of his belief in the journey of the soul and the ultimate peace found through communal living.

WEBSITES
Historic New Harmony, www.newharmony.org
Working Men's Institute Museum & Library,
    www.workingmensinstitute.org

NEARBY PLACES
The General George Patton Museum and Center of Leadership,
    www.generalpatton.org
Kentucky Derby Museum, www.derbymuseum.org
Lincoln Boyhood National Memorial, www.nps.gov/libo
Evansville Museum, www.emuseum.org

17

RAILROAD UNIVERSITY
OF THE UNITED STATES

BALTIMORE, MARYLAND

Mt. Clare Shops

On July 4, 1828, two groundbreaking ceremonies took place that offered contrasting visions of transportation in America. Just outside Washington, D.C., President John Quincy Adams attended the groundbreaking for the Chesapeake and Ohio (C&O) Canal, which would link the Potomac tidewater with the headwaters of the Ohio River. In Baltimore, Charles Carroll, the last living signer of the Declaration of Independence, laid the first stone of the Baltimore & Ohio (B&O) Railroad, which would connect Baltimore with the fast-developing Ohio River Valley over the Appalachians. During the next quarter century, the B&O and other rail lines overtook the competition that operated canals and turnpikes. Locomotives could operate wherever water and wood—coal by the 1880s—were available to keep boilers producing steam. In addition, a flanged train wheel, designed to better grip a rail, also lowered friction and made trains highly efficient and economical.

America did not invent the steam railroad. That distinction belonged to Great Britain. But the United States, with its large landmass and its population moving westward, quickly took the lead in railroad construction and train technology. By 1840, the United States had almost twice as many miles of track as all the nations of Europe combined. On the eve of the Civil War in 1861, a 30,000-mile network had been laid, three-quarters of it in the industrializing Northeast.

America's first railroad established a reputation for innovation. The B&O adopted the first steam locomotive made in America, built by Peter Cooper, a New York industrialist. Although his engine, the *Tom Thumb*, is reputed to have lost a race against a horse-drawn carriage, the B&O saw the advantages of steam power. The B&O also built the first stone viaduct and the first locomotive and railcar repair shops. The world's first telegraph, invented by Samuel Morse in 1844, ran along B&O right-of-way. The first railroad ticket and first timetable were B&O initiatives. By 1854, the B&O reached Wheeling, Virginia (now West Virginia), a distance twice as far as the C&O Canal over the same period. An engineering journal, noting the quality of annual reports, roads, and workshops, called the B&O the "Railroad University of the United States."

Railroads were the defining technology of the nineteenth century, changing every aspect of American life. Building railroads required unprecedented investment and an enormous workforce plus huge quantities of materials—iron and, later on, steel for locomotives and rails, timber for crossties, and wood or coal for fuel. Railroads created new towns and caused the rapid growth of cities. Farmers shifted production from diverse local subsistence to cash crops that could be shipped to distant markets by rail. California and Florida specialized in fresh fruit and vegetables that were shipped by iced refrigerator cars; the upper Midwest became America's granary; Texas, Oklahoma, and Kansas specialized in cattle, taken by the millions annually to midwestern slaughterhouses by train. Railroads changed concepts of space and time. A journey to California that once took five months by stagecoach or ship was now seven to ten days by train. To accommodate train schedules, first the railroads—and later Americans everywhere—adopted standard time and time zones.

In the Civil War, the North's advantages in industrial production, far more extensive railroad mileage, equipment, and skilled labor were decisive factors in defeating the South. During the war, Congress passed the Pacific Railroad Act to develop the West. The federal government offered land grants and loans to corporations to develop a transcontinental railroad, which was completed in 1869 with great ceremony at Promontory Summit, Utah.

The eighty-five years following the Civil War until just after WWII marked the high point of the railroads' growth and prosperity. By 1916, track mileage had grown to 254,000 and total investment reached $21 billion. More than 1.7 million people worked for railroads, which carried 77 percent of freight transport and 98 percent of passenger service between cities. During this period, industry leaders accumulated enormous fortunes and the names Vanderbilt, Stanford, Harriman, Hill, Morgan, Rockefeller, and Carnegie became synonymous with America's "Gilded Age."

Numerous inventions contributed to the railroad industry's success. Eli Janney's automatic knuckle coupler (1868) and George Westinghouse's air brakes (1869) increased safety for workers, passengers, and cargo. An African American inventor, Elijah McCoy, patented a mechanical lubricator (1872) for locomotives, an invention locomotive crews called "the Real McCoy" to signify its effectiveness.

The triumph of the railroads was not without consequence. Scandals such as the financial fraud called Crédit Mobilier nearly destroyed the Union Pacific Railroad in 1871 and implicated public officials. In 1877, a nationwide strike—the first such strike in U.S. history—began when the B&O cut wages, sparking violence that spread from Martinsburg, West Virginia, to Baltimore, Pittsburgh, Chicago, and St. Louis. American farmers formed the National Grange in 1867 to advocate for their economic rights against the exorbitant freight charges imposed by powerful railroads. The Grange's activism forced Congress to create the Interstate Commerce Commission in 1887 and to pass federal regulatory legislation.

Beginning in the mid-1930s, railroads declined economically, due mostly to competition from long-distance trucking. By the 1980s, trains provided only 36 percent of intercity freight transport and 3 percent of intercity passenger travel. The railroad industry's fortunes changed in 1980 when the Staggers Rail Act removed many old price restrictions and thus stimulated a dramatic freight railroad revival. Government-supported Amtrak was created by Congress in 1971 for passenger trains.

Railroad history enjoys a devoted following in America, and the B&O Railroad led the way in preserving this formative industry's heritage. At expositions in Philadelphia (1876) and Chicago (1893), railroads displayed original 1830s locomotives, and the B&O centennial celebration in 1927 drew 1.3 million people. In 1953, the B&O created the Baltimore & Ohio Railroad Museum at Mt. Clare Shops, the original site of the B&O's first locomotive and railcar repair facility. After the B&O became part of CSX Transportation in 1987, the museum continued as an independent institution. Located on a forty-acre campus in southwest Baltimore, the museum bills itself accurately as "the Birthplace of American Railroading" with significant historic buildings and an amazing collection of locomotives, rolling stock, and equipment. Educational programs appealing to families include train excursions to Mount Clare Museum House, the 1760s plantation of Charles Carroll, and to the Carrollton Viaduct (1829), an engineering marvel made of hand-set stone that still carries rail traffic today.

Another significant railroad building is the B&O Railroad Warehouse (1899), located behind Orioles Park at Camden Yards, designed by E. Francis Baldwin, one of the most productive architects in the mid-Atlantic region. Baldwin designed more than five hundred buildings, and most of his commissions came from the B&O Railroad and the Catholic Church. His masterpiece, the roundhouse at Mt. Clare Shops, is now the main exhibition building of the B&O Railroad Museum. Built in 1884, the roof was restored after a snowstorm in 2003 caused major damage. The roundhouse was once the world's largest circular industrial building—more than 135 feet tall and covering nearly an acre. It is a stunning example of beauty and functionality, its interior lit by natural light during the day. It is a tribute to Baldwin's dual passions of religion and design, truly deserving of its fame as a cathedral of industry.

WEBSITE
B&O Railroad Museum, www.borail.org

NEARBY PLACES
Fort McHenry National Monument and Historic Shrine, www.nps
    .gov/fomc

USS *Constellation*, www.historicships.org/constellation.html

The Star-Spangled Banner Flag House, www.flaghouse.org

Reginald F. Lewis Museum of Maryland African American History & Culture, www.lewismuseum.org

The Walters Art Museum, www.thewalters.org

18

THE ALAMO
SAN ANTONIO, TEXAS

The Alamo

Few historic sites in America are more famous than the Alamo, where as many as 257 men died in battle on March 6, 1836. The Alamo was the first of five missions established by Franciscan priests along the San Antonio River in the eighteenth century to re-create Spanish life on the colonial frontier with the goal of converting indigenous populations by providing instruction in the Catholic religion, farming, and ranching. The Spanish also protected mission Indians against hostile Indian groups and French settlers moving west from Louisiana. Originally known as the San Antonio de Valero Mission, the Alamo began operations in 1718 and construction began on the present chapel in 1756. The other missions included San José (1720) and three—San Juan, Concepción, and Espada—relocated from East Texas in 1731. In 1793, Spain secularized the missions and began moving troops into Texas. One military company, from a town south of the Rio Grande called Alamo de Parras, occupied the San Antonio de Valero Mission and, by the early nineteenth century, the former mission became known locally as "the Alamo."

The Battle of the Alamo took place during a rebellion in Coahuila y Tejas (now Texas), a Mexican state north of the Rio Grande River. After winning its independence from Spain in 1821, Mexico adopted a constitution in 1824 modeled on the U.S. Constitution. In 1834, however, President Antonio López de Santa Anna seized power, repudiated the federalist constitution, and named himself dictator, the "Napoléon of the West."

In Coahuila y Tejas, a resistance movement led by Stephen Austin sought greater autonomy from the central government in far-off Mexico City. Austin had promoted American settlement in Tejas and by the

1830s Anglos outnumbered Mexicans by 30,000 to 7,800. Most of these residents—Anglos and Mexicans—were *federalistas* and favored a return to constitutional government. In October 1835, they organized an army and successfully confronted Mexican forces in small skirmishes. In the Siege of Béxar at what is now San Antonio, the Texans forced a Mexican surrender. Embarrassed by this defeat, Santa Anna personally led his army into Texas in early 1836. By February, he was approaching the rebel stronghold in San Antonio.

As Santa Anna entered the city with two thousand soldiers, the rebels retreated across the San Antonio River into the Alamo. The old mission was in poor condition but the rebels managed to fortify themselves inside its four-foot-thick walls. Armed with several cannons, long rifles, and ammunition, they organized two units, veterans led by William Travis and volunteers led by Jim Bowie. Joining them was David (Davy) Crockett and the Tennessee volunteers. Crockett was a former congressman and author of a bestselling autobiography whose political career ended when he opposed President Andrew Jackson and voted against the Indian Removal Act of 1830, stating he could not stand against "the poor remnants of a once powerful people."

For twelve days, Santa Anna's artillery bombarded the mission and he demanded a full surrender. Travis refused and, in a letter "to all Texans," appealed for support with the defiant cry of "Victory or death!" The battle started before dawn on March 6 and lasted less than two hours. Santa Anna's forces killed nearly every man in the Alamo except for a few who were taken prisoner and later executed. His victory, however, came at a terrible price because the Alamo defenders killed around four hundred Mexicans and wounded many more. These losses proved decisive a few weeks later, when rebels led by Sam Houston defeated the Mexican army at the Battle of San Jacinto, securing independence for the Republic of Texas.

For nearly a decade, Texas was an independent nation. The annexation of Texas by the United States in 1845 was a major cause of the Mexican War from 1846 to 1848. Sam Houston served as governor of Texas but left office at the start of the Civil War after refusing to sign the act of secession in 1861 that made Texas a Confederate state.

After decades of neglect, the Alamo gained recognition as a historic landmark in the late nineteenth century. After the railroad reached San Antonio in 1875, the Alamo had become the city's major attraction. Its bell-shaped façade, or campanulate, added during renovations by the U.S. Army around 1850, became a symbol of freedom and independence. The plaza surrounding the former mission filled with commercial and retail establishments, hotels, and an opera house. At the same time, the Daughters of the Republic of Texas (DRT) adopted the Alamo as a symbol of the values and ideals of Texas's founders. For many years, they presented the site as an example of the triumph of Anglo over Mexican culture, reflecting their own racial attitudes rather than the realities of the independence movement. Two leaders of the DRT chapter that preserved the Alamo, Adina de Zavala and Claire Driscoll, fought commercial developers, the state of Texas, and even each other before the state agreed to purchase the site in 1905.

For more than a century, the DRT maintained vigorous control over the historical identity of the Alamo. At times, conflicts within the organization and between the DRT and the outside world—scholars, preservationists, tourism promoters—reached a level of intensity almost equal to the 1836 battle itself. Some of the controversies concern details about the battle that challenge cherished myths. For example, the enshrinement of the leaders of the Texas rebellion overlooks the bitter rivalries between Stephen Austin and Sam Houston and between William Travis and Jim Bowie. Even Davy Crockett, immortalized through films by Walt Disney and John Wayne, has faced the scrutiny of scholarship that suggests he may have surrendered and died at Santa Anna's command rather than in combat on a mission parapet. Although the DRT had opened the door slightly to new interpretations, the state of Texas recently has assumed greater control of the site. The door to the mission, however, still posts the DRT's Rules of Reverence and also a solemn request:

Be Silent Friend
Here Heroes Died
To Blaze a Trail
For Other Men

Visitors are surprised to find how small the Alamo appears today, a squat stone building surrounded by souvenir shops, commercial museums, and restaurants. Tourism has triumphed at the Alamo. Yet evidence of San Antonio's rich history survives, including the plazas and streets of the seventeenth-century Spanish plan. The National Park Service manages four of the five eighteenth-century missions, which continue to be active Catholic parishes. These missions, along with the Alamo, are now UNESCO World Heritage Sites. San Antonio is also the site of River Walk, a linear park planned in the 1920s that complements the city's historic preservation movement.

Though the Alamo stands, little else remains from the war for Texas independence. It is still possible, with a knowledgeable guide, to identify the sites associated with Santa Anna's siege and reconstruct the course of a brutal battle. On East Commerce Street, a short walk from the historic mission, a plaque marks the site of two funeral pyres where the defenders—Anglos and Mexicans—were cremated. That horrific scene survives in our imaginations, a haunting reminder of the epic struggle that took place here in the formative years of an expanding nation.

WEBSITES
The Alamo, www.thealamo.org
San Antonio Missions National Historical Park, www.nps.gov/saan

NEARBY PLACES
The San Antonio River Walk, www.thesanantonioriverwalk.com
The Witte Museum, www.wittemuseum.org

19

DECLARATION OF SENTIMENTS

SENECA FALLS, NEW YORK

Wesleyan Chapel

A small chapel in an upstate New York factory town was an unlikely setting for the world's first convention on women's rights. Yet because of the powerful leadership of Elizabeth Cady Stanton and her allies, three hundred people—women and men—gathered there on July 19 and 20, 1848, and adopted a document, the Declaration of Sentiments, that has become a touchstone of American democracy. Stanton's home in Seneca Falls is part of a national historic park that includes the Wesleyan Chapel, the site of the convention, and two homes in nearby Waterloo—the M'Clintock House, where convention organizers met, and the Hunt House, where they drafted the Declaration of Sentiments. Along with the home of famous Underground Railroad conductor Harriet Tubman in nearby Auburn, these places are reminders of the close connection between the women's rights and abolition movements and the continuing struggle for human rights today.

The Women's Rights Convention of 1848 took place through the initiative of Stanton and Lucretia Mott, a Quaker minister and social activist from Philadelphia. They had met in 1840 at the World's Anti-Slavery Convention in London. When the convention's leaders refused to allow women to participate in its deliberations, Stanton and Mott agreed they needed to address the cause of women's rights. Stanton later wrote that "the action of this convention . . . stung many women into new thought and action and gave rise to the movement for women's political equality in England and in the United States." The two women renewed their friendship in July 1848 when Mott was visiting Waterloo, a few miles from Stanton's home in Seneca Falls. They decided to act on the idea that they had discussed in London eight years earlier. They agreed to convene at Wesleyan Chapel, built a few years earlier, which had become a gathering place for abolitionists, pacifist groups, and temperance societies.

With only two weeks to prepare, they boldly announced that "a Convention to discuss the social, civil, and religious condition and rights of women, will be held in the Wesleyan Chapel, in Seneca Falls, N.Y." Three days before the convention, they drafted a document modeled on the Declaration of Independence proclaiming that "all men and women are created equal." The Declaration of Sentiments had eleven goals, the most ambitious—and controversial—being provision number nine: "Resolved, that it is the duty of the women of this country to secure to themselves their sacred right to the elective franchise."

On July 19, hundreds of women attended the convention that featured a rousing speech by Lucretia Mott. The next day, men joined the deliberations and the convention adopted the Declaration of Sentiments in its entirety. One hundred people—sixty-eight women and thirty-two men—signed the document, including Stanton, Mott, Frederick Douglass, and other advocates of social and political reform.

Elizabeth Cady Stanton, born in Johnstown, New York, in 1815, had come of age during a period of enormous change in America, a period shaped by the religious revivals of the Second Great Awakening, the politics of Jacksonian democracy, the philosophy of transcendentalism, and various reform movements that swept across the country. The family influences in her life included her father, a prominent jurist and professor; her cousin Gerrit Smith, a national leader in the abolitionist movement; and her husband, Henry Stanton, also an abolitionist. The Stantons celebrated their honeymoon by attending the 1840 antislavery conference in London, where she met Lucretia Mott.

No cause was more central to these times than the abolition of slavery. Criticism of slavery was not new, but two events in 1831—Nat Turner's rebellion in Virginia and William Lloyd Garrison's publication of the antislavery newspaper *The Liberator* in Boston—generated greater attention to the issue. Garrison's defiant declaration "I am in earnest—I will not equivocate—I will not excuse—I will not retreat a single inch—AND I WILL BE HEARD" was a clarion call to action. For the next thirty years, the debate over how to end slavery in the United States preoccupied America's political life.

The slavery issue overshadowed concerns about women's rights. Yet the second-class status of women was clearly evident. Women could not vote or hold office. They could not go to college, and if they were married, they could not enter into contracts or work outside the home. It was rare for a woman even to speak in public. The Grimké sisters, Sarah and Angelina, stirred controversy in the 1830s when they began making public speeches to mixed audiences of men and women at antislavery gatherings. The Grimkés, Margaret Fuller, and their colleagues forged a social and intellectual network that became a powerful voice for women's rights.

The impact of the Seneca Falls Convention faded during the Civil War and Reconstruction, but the issue of women's rights never disappeared from public view. Elizabeth Cady Stanton continued her advocacy, attracting allies like Susan B. Anthony, also a New Yorker. Stanton died in 1902 before achieving her lifetime goal of political equality. In 1920, the Nineteenth Amendment to the U.S. Constitution finally passed, granting voting rights to women.

It is noteworthy that Harriet Tubman purchased her home from William Seward, former New York governor, U.S. senator, and secretary of state in Lincoln's cabinet. Seward's well-preserved home in Auburn, also an Underground Railroad site, is open for public tours. These places and the sites at Seneca Falls commemorate alliances that transcended race, gender, and partisan politics at a time when Americans were still defining democracy. Who would participate in America's politics? Who had the right to be a citizen? The Seneca Falls women's rights convention provided an answer, but the questions are still relevant today.

NATIONAL PARK SERVICE

Elizabeth Cady Stanton House

WEBSITES

Women's Rights National Historical Park, www.nps.gov/wori
Harriet Tubman Home, www.harriethouse.org
Seward House Historic Museum, www.sewardhouse.org

NEARBY PLACES

John Brown Farm State Historic Site, www.nysparks.com/historic
    -sites/29/details.aspx
Joseph Smith Farm, www.hillcumorah.org/welcomectr.php
National Susan B. Anthony Museum & House,
    www.susanbanthonyhouse.org

20

TEMPLE SQUARE

SALT LAKE CITY, UTAH

The Mormon Tabernacle

Each year on July 24, Utah observes Pioneer Day, commemorating the Mormon pioneers' entrance into the Great Salt Lake valley in 1847. That day marked the culmination of a dramatic and often controversial period that began in the 1820s, when Joseph Smith founded the Church of Jesus Christ of Latter-day Saints, commonly called the Mormon Church or LDS Church. Starting with just six members in 1830, the church has grown to become a popular and powerful institution with more than fifteen million members worldwide and six million members in the United States in 2010. While several religions have started in the United States, the Church of Jesus Christ of Latter-day Saints is unique because it is the only one whose story of origin takes place in America.

According to Smith, an angel named Moroni directed him to a book made of golden tablets in a field near his home in Palmyra, New York. Smith translated the text on these plates into the Book of Mormon, the history of a people said to be a lost tribe of Israel, who settled in America around 600 BC and were among the ancestors of the American Indians. The main narrator of the book, the prophet Nephi, recounts the passage of the tribe across the ocean, their settlement in America, and a visit by Jesus Christ before his ascension to heaven. Christ's mission ushered in a period of peace in America followed by warfare that left only the prophet Mormon and his son, Moroni, as survivors.

Some critics, like Mark Twain, have scoffed at the Book of Mormon as "a tedious plagiarism of the New Testament." Whatever its shortcomings as literature, the mere existence of the Book of Mormon, a written text that commanded authority, was a powerful factor in attracting converts.

The Mormons, or Latter-day Saints, as they prefer to be called, emerged during a period historians call America's Second Great Awakening, a time of religious revival in response to industrialization, political division, and social reform. Their home in upstate New York was known as the "burnt over district," where numerous sects and utopian communities emerged in the late 1820s and 1830s, often attracting firestorms of controversy.

The Latter-day Saints were among those groups that immediately stirred resistance. As Smith continued to report new visions and revelations, the Mormons adopted doctrines and practices that put them in conflict with other religions, government authorities, and even with each other. For example, their practice of polygamy—plural marriage—offended the morality of most Americans. The belief in proxy baptism on behalf of those who have died alienated many non-Mormons who did not consent to baptizing their ancestors. Mormon theology rejected the idea of the Trinity, the unity of God the Father, Jesus the Son, and the Holy Spirit, believing instead that God and Jesus are separate physical beings. Furthermore, their doctrine of "exaltation" taught that after death human beings could become godlike, an idea that appeared to equate humankind with the Creator. These beliefs and the missionary zeal with which the Mormons recruited new members caused opposition from other denominations.

To avoid conflicts with his neighbors in Palmyra, Smith moved his congregation to Kirtland, Ohio, in 1831. At the same time, he promoted a settlement in Independence, Missouri, where he hoped to create New Jerusalem, a holy city where the Messiah would return to earth. In 1837, he moved to Independence, but within two years, the Mormon presence created such fierce resistance that Missouri's governor issued an executive order known as the "Extermination Order," expelling Smith and the Mormons.

Their next stop was Nauvoo, Illinois, where they built an impressive Greek Revival temple decorated with cosmic symbols—sunstones, moonstones, and starstones—representative of their faith in the afterlife.

They also secured enormous political and economic power. Just as it appeared they had found a permanent home, an internal struggle within the church led to the arrest of Smith and his brother, Hyrum. On June 27, 1844, a mob stormed the jail where they were held and murdered them both.

To succeed their martyred founder, the Mormons rallied around Brigham Young, one of Smith's apostles who had recruited thousands of converts to the church, including poor English mill workers. Convinced that the Mormons needed to settle outside the boundaries of the United States, Young led a mass migration that began in 1845, an epic 1,500-mile journey that ended in 1847 in the arid valley surrounding the Great Salt Lake. The rapid growth of the new colony they called Deseret is one of the great chapters in the history of the American West.

By the late 1850s, Brigham Young controlled a huge territory that included what is now all of Utah and parts of Arizona, Nevada, Wyoming, and Idaho. He and his circle of church elders had, in effect, created an independent theocracy that challenged the basic principle of the separation of church and state as well as the authority of the U.S. government. In 1857, President James Buchanan sent troops to Deseret to assert federal power. Although no battles took place in the so-called Mormon War, there were occasional clashes and casualties. The most violent episode took place on September 11, 1857, when a Mormon militia massacred 120 men, women, and children pioneers en route to California at a site in southwestern Utah called Mountain Meadows. After a year of negotiations, Young acknowledged the supremacy of the federal government and agreed to step down as territorial governor.

Over the ensuing decades, the Mormons became less isolated and gained greater acceptance. They established successful businesses, educational institutions, and an extensive genealogical library. They developed a productive farming economy and earned praise from conservationists like John Wesley Powell for their irrigation techniques in the high desert. They also abandoned the practice of plural marriage, a decision that paved the way for Utah to achieve statehood in 1896.

A visit to Temple Square in the state capital of Salt Lake City is the best way to understand the history of the Latter-day Saints. The ten-acre complex includes the Salt Lake Temple, the Church History Museum, and the Mormon Tabernacle, called "an architectural masterpiece" by Frank Lloyd Wright. While only Mormons may enter the main temple, all the other sites, exhibitions, art displays, gardens, and parks are open for public tours without charge.

About a mile east of Temple Square, the University of Utah recently opened the Natural History Museum of Utah, a stunning facility with views of the Wasatch Mountains and an extraordinary collection of dinosaur fossils, geological specimens, and cultural artifacts of Native Americans. These exhibitions offer a radically different version of history from the spiritual adventure found in the Book of Mormon. The temple and the museum provide dramatic evidence of the tension between faith and science, a tension that has tested the ideals of religious and intellectual freedom in American history.

WEBSITE
Temple Square, www.templesquare.com

NEARBY PLACES
Natural History Museum of Utah, www.nhmu.utah.edu
Church History Museum, www.history.lds.org/section
    /museum?lang=eng
Fort Douglas Military Museum, www.fortdouglas.org

21

FORT SUMTER

CHARLESTON, SOUTH CAROLINA

Fort Sumter

On the day after Confederate artillery fired on the federal fort in Charleston harbor, Jonathan Dillon, a young Irish immigrant, was cleaning the gold pocket watch of President Abraham Lincoln in a Washington shop. Before finishing his work, Dillon engraved a message in the watch that Fort Sumter in Charleston, South Carolina, "was attacked by the rebels," adding a postscript: "thank God we have a government."

Lincoln never saw Dillon's message but he carried the watch and the burden of sustaining a fragile nation through four years of war that began on April 12, 1861. For more than a decade, major events—the Fugitive Slave Act (1850); the publication of *Uncle Tom's Cabin* (1852) by Harriet Beecher Stowe; the Kansas-Nebraska Act (1854), which endorsed the doctrine of popular sovereignty; Bleeding Kansas (1854–58), which foreshadowed bitter violence over slavery; the Supreme Court's Dred Scott decision (1857), which denied the rights of citizenship to African Americans; John Brown's raid on the federal arsenal in Harpers Ferry (1859)—fueled a sectional conflict that led to an inevitable military confrontation.

No event in this timeline, however, loomed larger than the presidential election of 1860. Four candidates representing sectional and ideological differences revealed deep and irreconcilable divisions. The Republican Party, formed in 1854 in reaction to the Kansas-Nebraska Act, selected Abraham Lincoln to lead its ticket. Although he had not held elected office since 1848, Lincoln had built a national reputation as a skilled speaker and thoughtful advocate of national unity. He was not an abolitionist but opposed the expansion of slavery in the West.

Lincoln won the election with less than 40 percent of the popular vote and not a single electoral vote from the South. Reaction to his election came swiftly as Southerners calculated the risks—economic, political, social, and cultural—that a Lincoln presidency represented. Within weeks after the election, South Carolina's leaders convened in Charleston and voted to leave the union. By February 1861, seven states had seceded and formed a new nation, the Confederate States of America. They adopted a constitution and elected Jefferson Davis president.

When Lincoln took the oath of office on March 4, 1861, he faced a crisis unlike any other in American history. In his inaugural address he made the case for unity and declared that "we must not be enemies." He appealed to "the mystic chords of memory" that bound the nation together and to "the better angels of our nature" that would avert a war.

His words were eloquent but they came too late. Once in office, Lincoln had to respond to the Southern demand that the United States give up all its property in the new Confederacy. One of those properties was Fort Sumter. This massive brick structure, with walls forty feet high and twelve feet thick, was still under construction in 1860 when Major Robert Anderson and his unit of eighty-five soldiers moved in. Although Anderson was from Kentucky and sympathized with the South, he refused to give up the fort and called for support from Washington. Lincoln did not want to be accused of starting a war and sent a ship with food and other necessities without weapons or ammunition, probably knowing even this action would provoke the South to attack.

He was right. On April 12, while citizens of Charleston watched in amazement from the rooftops of their homes, Confederate artillery began a thirty-four-hour assault. Major Anderson mounted a spirited defense but he was outgunned and outmanned. Although none of his men were killed during the attack, the fort sustained substantial damage and the supply ship never reached its destination.

Anderson's surrender on April 14 touched off a wave of outrage and patriotism in the North. Lincoln called for 75,000 volunteers to put down the Southern rebellion, prompting four more Southern states to secede. The Civil War, a conflict that would last four years and result in the deaths of 750,000 men on both sides, had begun.

After the war began, Charleston was on the periphery of major battle action. In 1863, however, Union troops turned their attention to Charleston as a target, both for its strategic importance and as a symbol of Southern resistance. The first attacks came in July 1863 and continued for nearly two years. Among the units in this campaign was the 54th Massachusetts Volunteer Infantry Regiment, comprising African American soldiers and led by their white commander, Colonel Robert Gould Shaw. (See page 39.) The 54th Regiment suffered heavy losses trying to capture Fort Wagner and Colonel Shaw died in the battle. This unit and the 180,000 African Americans who served in the Union army won high praise for their discipline and courage.

The Union army finally captured Fort Sumter and Charleston in February 1865, just before the war ended. After the war, the U.S. Army rebuilt the fort and installed a lighthouse station and artillery batteries there. In 1948, the National Park Service assumed responsibility for the fort's preservation and now offers guided tours of Fort Sumter and other Civil War sites in Charleston harbor.

The city of Charleston itself is an essential stop on anyone's tour of America's historic sites. Its splendid architecture includes residential, religious, and public landmarks of the eighteenth and nineteenth centuries. Well-preserved plantations such as Drayton Hall and Middleton Place, a few miles from the city, offer visitors an excellent introduction to antebellum life. Of less architectural importance but highly significant for its history is the Old Slave Mart on the cobblestoned Chalmers Street, a private indoor marketplace established in 1859 after the city prohibited public slave trading. In 1938, a local preservationist, Miriam Wilson, bought and restored the market as a museum, an early example of a historic site of conscience. One mile north of the Old Slave Mart is the historic Emanuel African Methodist Episcopal Church (1891) that became another symbol of America's tragic racial history when nine church members were murdered during a prayer meeting on June 17, 2015.

More than anywhere else in America, Fort Sumter, the Old Slave Mart, and the river plantations provide vivid and dramatic evidence of the connection between slavery and the Civil War. Lincoln articulated this connection in his Second Inaugural Address on March 4, 1865. He noted that slavery was "a peculiar and powerful interest. All knew that this interest was the cause of the war." He appealed for an end to the war and for reconciliation: "With malice toward none, with charity toward all, let us bind up the nation's wounds." Lincoln did not live to shape the peace he envisioned. On April 15, three days after the South surrendered, he died from an assassin's bullet, unaware of the prayer for the nation engraved in his gold watch.

WEBSITES

Fort Sumter National Monument, www.nps.gov/fosu

Old Slave Mart, www.nps.gov/nr/travel/charleston/osm.htm

Emanuel African Methodist Episcopal Church,
    www.emanuelamechurch.org

NEARBY PLACES

Drayton Hall, www.draytonhall.org

Middleton Place, www.middletonplace.org

The Charleston Museum, www.charlestonmuseum.org

22

NEW BIRTH OF FREEDOM

GETTYSBURG, PENNSYLVANIA

Gettysburg Seminary Ridge Museum

On July 1, 1863, Gettysburg's Lutheran Theological Seminary served as a command post for Brigadier General John Buford, the Union officer credited with holding back the advancing Confederate army and securing a defensive position on the high ground south of town. Today, this building is the Seminary Ridge Museum, where visitors can climb to the cupola and see the battlefield as Buford saw it. The museum documents the heroic but crude methods used to treat wounded soldiers when the seminary became a field hospital during and after the battle. And visitors learn about the response of Lutherans and other churches to the divisive issue of slavery. In town along Baltimore Street, the Shriver House Museum presents the experience of one family that fled for safety while Confederate soldiers occupied their home and where a makeshift hospital cared for wounded Union troops in the weeks following the battle. Clearly, the small town of Gettysburg (population 2,400) was as much a battle zone as the ten thousand acres of hills and fields that surround it.

When General Robert E. Lee and his Army of Northern Virginia entered Pennsylvania in June 1863, their goal was to demoralize the North and capture the strategically important town of Harrisburg, the state capital and railroad center. Fresh from victories at Fredericksburg and Chancellorsville, Lee and his generals—Longstreet, Hill, Ewell, Pettigrew, and Pickett—were confident that the North, disorganized and poorly led, could not resist an invasion. They might even surrender, sue for peace, and recognize the Confederacy as an independent nation.

Lee and his army of 70,000 men encountered Northern troops on June 30, and fighting began the next morning. By the end of July 1, the

South occupied Gettysburg and had forced the North to retreat to a defensive line along Cemetery Ridge and neighboring Culp's Hill, a line called "the fishhook" by the troops. That evening Union commander Major General George Meade brought a large force of troops. Now the North had superior numbers—an army of 93,000 men—and access to supplies from nearby towns and farms.

On July 2 Confederates attacked the left and right flanks of Meade's army. The fighting often involved hand-to-hand combat and lasted for hours. The fields and hills—the Wheatfield, the Peach Orchard, Little Round Top—became scenes of violent death. The Southern assault only partially succeeded as Union troops held their ground and regrouped for another battle. The following day Lee ordered a two-hour artillery bombardment from Seminary Ridge, where Confederate troops were located, then sent more than 12,000 Confederate infantry on a one-mile march across open fields directly into Union lines. This daring attack, known in history as Pickett's Charge, failed to dislodge the North. At the same time, a fierce cavalry battle raged four miles east of town as 3,000 Union soldiers, including a Michigan unit led by Brigadier General George Custer, turned back an attack by 4,500 Confederates under the command of Major J. E. B. Stuart. The North defended its positions and its home territory, forcing Lee's troops into a humiliating retreat. The victory at Gettysburg, coupled with the capture of Vicksburg, Mississippi, by General Ulysses S. Grant on July 4, was a turning point in a conflict that nearly destroyed the nation. Although the war lasted almost two more years, the North's overwhelming advantages in men, weapons, transportation, and communication proved decisive.

More than 7,000 men died in the Battle of Gettysburg, about the same number from each side. Another 44,000 men were wounded or missing in action. The battle had resulted in more casualties than any in American history. The massive destruction and carnage on the battlefield required an extraordinary relief and repair effort. Medical teams directed by Dr. Jonathan Letterman and a corps of nurses cared for the sick and wounded in makeshift hospitals. Pennsylvania governor Andrew Gregg

Curtin organized a massive cleanup, cremating more than 5,000 horses, shipping 3,200 Confederate dead by rail to the South, and reburying 3,500 Union dead in a new Soldiers National Cemetery near the "High Water Mark," the scene of the final moments of combat.

When President Lincoln arrived on November 19 to dedicate the National Cemetery, the ceremony offered him an opportunity to pay tribute to the loyalty and sacrifice of federal soldiers. As he honored the men who died in battle, he also transformed their sacrifice into a statement about the meaning of the American experience. Inspired by his extensive reading of the Bible, Shakespeare, and the nation's founding documents, he cited core values—liberty, equality, freedom, and self-government. He predicted that "this nation shall have a new birth of freedom" and redefined the Civil War as a conflict not only to preserve the Union but also to end slavery.

Millions of visitors have followed in Lincoln's footsteps to see the battlefields of Gettysburg. Veterans from both sides placed more than 1,300 monuments to mark where they fought and their comrades fell. The tourist industry grew so large that it threatened at times to replace the sites of battle action with motels, restaurants, and souvenir shops. In spite of development pressures and occasional clashes between commercial and commemorative interests, the U.S. Army and later the National Park Service have preserved Gettysburg's most significant landmarks. One of the most prominent preservation advocates was President Dwight Eisenhower, who served in Gettysburg during World War I as commander of Camp Colt, the Army's Tank Corps training center, located where Pickett's Charge took place. In retirement, he and his wife, Mamie, made Gettysburg their home, and after his death their farm became part of the national park.

A new museum and visitor center (2008) is the starting point for a visit to Gettysburg. Exhibitions, films, and a first-rate bookstore offer a comprehensive introduction to the battle and the war. The Cyclorama, a monumental 360-degree painting by Paul Philippoteaux (1884), depicts the final day of the battle accompanied by a sound and light show.

Exploring the battlefield itself, either with a licensed guide or on a self-guided tour, offers new insights into this epic event. In addition to the most popular sites, it is worthwhile to spend some quiet moments in the more remote sections of the park, such as Culp's Hill and East Cavalry Field. In the National Cemetery rows of stone markers and metal plaques with lines from "The Bivouac of the Dead" by Theodore O'Hara bear witness to the tragic ends of war.

WEBSITES
Gettysburg National Military Park, www.nps.gov/gett
Eisenhower National Historic Site, www.nps.gov/eise
East Cavalry Field, www.civilwar.org/battlefields/gettysburg/maps
    /eastcavalryfieldmap.html

NEARBY PLACES
Gettysburg Black History Museum, www.gettysburgblackhistory.org
Shriver House Museum, www.shriverhouse.org
Seminary Ridge Museum, www.seminaryridgemuseum.org

23

SCHOOLHOUSE AND
FIELDHOUSE

MANHATTAN AND LAWRENCE, KANSAS

Anderson Hall, Kansas State University

In the middle of the Civil War, when the future of the United States was still in doubt, an activist Congress passed several laws in 1862 that built a modern nation. The Homestead Act made it possible for Americans of all backgrounds, including immigrants, to become landowners. The Pacific Railway Act encouraged construction of the transcontinental railroad. And the Morrill Act created universities in every state that would prepare students for careers in farming and engineering.

The author of the last bill, Representative Justin Smith Morrill of Vermont, was concerned that a college education in the United States was available only to an elite class at private schools that taught classical languages, history, literature, and philosophy. His bill provided a formula for allocating federal land to every state—30,000 acres for each senator and representative—to generate funding for "land grant colleges" that would offer a "practical" curriculum, especially subjects that would advance and sustain economic growth. President Lincoln signed the Morrill Act in 1862 and also approved legislation creating the U.S. Department of Agriculture.

For the past 150 years, land grant colleges have met a variety of economic and social needs. In 1890, at a time when racial segregation prevailed in the South, a second Morrill Act provided support for schools for African Americans. Not until 1992, however, were American Indian colleges extended membership in this network. Congress also expanded the mission of land grant colleges by authorizing experimental research stations in 1887 and agricultural extension services in 1914, which offered information and training to farmers.

The growth of land grant colleges coincided with the phenomenal

Allen Fieldhouse, University of Kansas

rise of productivity on America's farms. By the early twentieth century, agriculture became a major national industry, thanks in large measure to the work ethic and resilience of farmers and their families. Their ability to exploit favorable soils and climate and to utilize an array of new machinery—planters, plows, harvesters, and, on larger farms, combines— contributed to astounding productivity. The emergence of agricultural corporations like John Deere, Caterpillar, Armour, and General Mills marked the beginning of agribusiness. Later in the twentieth century, Cargill, Monsanto, ADM, and Bunge became powerful global corporations. Nevertheless, the overwhelming majority of farms in Kansas and the rest of America remained family owned.

Kansas State University, known statewide as K-State, was the first fully operational college created under the Morrill Act. In 1863, the state legislature chartered the school on the grounds of Bluemont Central College in the town of Manhattan. The first class of fifty-two students enrolled with an equal number of women and men. By the late 1870s, K-State gained a reputation for quality programs in agricultural science, chemistry, and engineering.

Anderson Hall, built from 1879 to 1884, has served as the university's administrative center and the office of every K-State president since John A. Anderson, for whom it is named. It is a handsome Queen Anne–style masonry building with a five-story central tower that still dominates the university, which consists of 23,500 students and nine colleges spread out over 668 acres. A tour of the campus includes the Hale Library, with an excellent rare-book collection; the Beach Museum of Art, featuring local and regional artists; and a botanical garden.

Less than two hours' drive east of K-State is the University of Kansas (KU) in Lawrence, where in 1856 John Brown and a small band of abolitionists faced off against proslavery Missourians. This episode in the conflict known as "Bleeding Kansas" foreshadowed the Civil War. During the war, William Quantrill and a band of Confederate raiders destroyed nearly every business and many houses in the town. The university, founded in 1866, emerged during postwar reconstruction. By the late nineteenth century, KU had more than one thousand students.

The arrival of James Naismith in 1898 transformed KU into a national center for the new sport of basketball. Naismith had invented the game at a YMCA training school in Springfield, Massachusetts, in 1891 as a form of winter recreation. He came to KU as a chapel director and physical education instructor, and became the school's first basketball coach, the only coach in KU history with a losing lifetime record (56 wins, 60 losses). His best player, Forrest "Phog" Allen, succeeded Naismith as coach in 1909. Known as the father of basketball coaching,

Monroe Elementary School

Allen's players included Adolph Rupp and Dean Smith, who became Hall of Fame coaches at Kentucky and North Carolina, respectively. Allen won a national championship in 1952 and the university named a new arena for him that opened in 1954.

Allen Fieldhouse, located on Naismith Drive, is a major landmark of America's sports history. Even after a recent renovation, the arena retains a traditional atmosphere and the spirit of its rural midwestern setting. On Saturday afternoons and cold winter nights, 16,300 fans file past a banner warning "Pay heed all who enter: Beware of the Phog" and chant in unison, "Rock Chalk, Jay Hawk, KU." Adjacent to the area is the Booth Family Hall of Athletics, a new museum with displays about Naismith, Allen, and the NCAA championship teams coached by Larry Brown (1988) and Bill Self (2008). There is also a wonderful exhibit about Wilt Chamberlain, who played at "The Phog" from 1955 to 1957. A superb athlete and arguably the greatest player ever, he was also one of the first African Americans to play at a major midwestern school. The museum will soon house the original copy of Naismith's Thirteen Rules of Basketball and secure KU's claim as the sport's capital.

Within a short drive of K-State and KU are several important museums and historic sites. In Topeka, the Brown v. Board of Education National Historic Site, located in the former Monroe Elementary School, provides an excellent overview of the civil rights movement and the Supreme Court case that ended the doctrine of "separate but equal" in public schools. The libraries of two presidents—Harry Truman in Independence, Missouri, and Dwight Eisenhower in Abilene, Kansas, are within an hour's drive of Topeka.

Not far from Manhattan, in the town of Wamego, is the OZ Museum, an impressive collection devoted to Frank Baum's series of children's books and the films, plays, games, and memorabilia that have sustained the popularity of *The Wonderful Wizard of Oz*—an original American fairy tale—for more than a century. The contrast between the fantasy of the Emerald City and the reality of Dorothy's farm inspired her to say that "we're not in Kansas anymore," a sentiment that rings true even today.

WEBSITES

Kansas State University, www.k-state.edu

University of Kansas, Booth Family Hall of Athletics, www.kuathletics
.com/boothhall

OZ Museum, www.ozmuseum.com

NEARBY PLACES

Brown v. Board of Education National Historic Site, www.nps.gov
/brvb

Dwight D. Eisenhower Presidential Library, Museum and Boyhood
Home, www.eisenhower.archives.gov

Harry S. Truman Library and Museum, www.trumanlibrary.org

24

FIRST NATIONAL PARK

YELLOWSTONE NATIONAL PARK, WYOMING

The Roosevelt Arch

"Thousands of tired, nerve-shaken, over-civilized people are beginning to find out that going to the mountains is going home; that wildness is a necessity; and that mountain parks and reservations are useful not only as fountains of timber and irrigating rivers, but as fountains of life" (John Muir, *Our National Parks*, 1901).

National parks are an American invention. With a few exceptions, the nobility in Europe and Asia—kings and emperors, lords and dukes—controlled access by ordinary citizens to land for recreation. In the United States, the policy of maintaining publicly owned land appealed to the values of a democratic society. Boston Common (1634), Philadelphia's Fairmount Park (1855), and New York's Central Park (1859) are good examples of public space set aside for recreation and as retreats from the crowded conditions of urban life.

The idea that the federal government should protect public land grew in the nineteenth century. In 1832, George Catlin, renowned for his portraits of American Indians, feared westward expansion would destroy their civilization and proposed a "nation's park, containing man and beast, in all the wild[ness] and freshness of their nature's beauty." As the industrial revolution, powered by the steam engine and the railroad, swept across the country, writers and artists such as Henry David Thoreau and Thomas Cole, respectively, raised public awareness of America's unique landscapes.

While the Civil War preoccupied the nation, advocates for preserving California's Yosemite Valley prevailed upon Congress and President Lincoln in 1864 to transfer some federally owned lands to the state "for public use . . . inalienable for all time." One of the commissioners appointed to manage Yosemite, the renowned landscape architect Frederick

Law Olmsted, wrote that the valley represented "greater glory of nature . . . the union of the deepest sublimity with the deepest beauty." Following the war, reports of the natural wonders of the American West generated more enthusiasm for federal action in wilderness protection. John Wesley Powell's explorations on the Colorado River in 1869 and 1871 and his description of the Grand Canyon riveted the nation. In 1868, John Muir moved to Yosemite and subsequently publicized the need for additional government protection. During this same period, three expeditions to Montana and Wyoming territories provided vivid accounts of the remarkable geology and fantastic sites of the Yellowstone Valley, especially its hot springs and geysers that spouted steam hundreds of feet in the air.

Other factors—completion of the transcontinental railroad, exploration for gold and other minerals, and continued conflict with Indians over territorial rights—created pressure for federal action to protect public lands in the West. With active lobbying by the Northern Pacific Railway and other tourism promoters, Congress passed legislation in 1872 establishing Yellowstone National Park, two million acres in Wyoming, Montana, and Idaho, "for the benefit and enjoyment of the people." The law also authorized the secretary of the interior to "prevent wanton destruction" and to "provide for the preservation, from injury or spoliation, of all timber, mineral deposits, natural curiosities, or wonders . . . and their retention in their natural condition." It was the first time in world history that a national government had taken such a bold action.

In reality, Yellowstone had little protection. For more than a decade, the park suffered an invasion of hunters, trappers, and souvenir collectors. Tourist camp operators, encouraged by the Northern Pacific, set up illegal commercial bathhouses at the hot springs. Without funding from Congress, park managers had to turn to the U.S. Army for protection. In 1886, General Philip Sheridan, a Civil War veteran and Indian fighter, dispatched cavalry to patrol the park. Fort Yellowstone was the headquarters for an operation that involved as many as three hundred soldiers. It continued until the National Park Service took over in 1918. The distinctive uniforms of rangers at national parks reflect this military heritage.

Old Faithful

John Muir's influence on the national parks movement was crucial. His family had emigrated from Scotland to Wisconsin, where he studied botany and geology at the University of Wisconsin. He avidly read the Bible, committed whole passages to memory, and drew inspiration from the writings of the New England transcendentalists. After settling in Yosemite, he explored the valley, published articles encouraging its preservation, and gave tours for visitors, including the philosopher Ralph Waldo Emerson in 1871.

Muir's activism resulted in Yosemite's designation as a national park in 1890. Two years later, he founded the Sierra Club, dedicated to protecting Yosemite and later a preeminent conservation organization. His 1901 publication, *Our National Parks*, made a passionate case for federal action. When he hosted President Theodore Roosevelt at Yosemite in 1903, he persuaded the president to support the conservation movement. Roosevelt expanded Yosemite, added three more areas as national parks, and signed the Antiquities Act (1906), which gave the president the authority to protect cultural, natural, and scientific treasures on public lands as national monuments.

The most famous battle in Muir's career came not with developers but with a fellow conservationist, Gifford Pinchot. Appointed the first director of the U.S. Forest Service in 1898, Pinchot believed that the best way to conserve natural resources was to manage them for profit. He also favored construction of a reservoir in Hetch Hetchy Valley, a Yosemite Park site, to provide water for San Francisco. In spite of bitter opposition led by Muir, Congress and President Wilson approved the project in 1913.

Even in defeat Muir attracted new recruits to his cause, most notably Stephen Mather, a wealthy California businessman who devoted his fortune to promoting national parks and a federal agency to manage them. In 1916, the Sierra Club, the General Federation of Women's Clubs, and leading progressives like Mather and Horace McFarland of Pennsylvania lobbied Congress to create the National Park Service with Mather its first director. He used his personal wealth to purchase parkland and often paid park staff out of his own pocket.

Today, there are 58 national parks and nearly 350 monuments, memorials, battlefields, and recreation areas in the National Park Service system. Yellowstone remains one of the largest and one of the most complex to manage. For example, forest fires, not uncommon during the dry summer season, can rage out of control, as in 1988, when nine separate fires affected almost 800,000 acres—36 percent of the park. Equally challenging is the need to maintain a balance between the park's wildlife—grizzly bears, bison, wolves, and elk—and rare plant life. Finally, there are the demands of the public—three million tourists annually—who flock to Yellowstone to see its world-renowned collection of geysers, colored hot springs, bubbling mud spots, and fumaroles (steam vents). Preserving this fragile environment, what John Muir called "the blessed old Yellowstone Wonderland," is no less a task today than when Americans first discovered its extraordinary beauty.

WEBSITE
Yellowstone National Park, www.nps.gov/yell

NEARBY PLACES
Fort Yellowstone and cabins built by the U.S. Army, www.nps.gov/yell
/learn/historyculture/fortyellowstone.htm
Museum of the American West, www.museumoftheamericanwest.com

25

NOOK FARM NEIGHBORS: STOWE AND TWAIN

HARTFORD, CONNECTICUT

The Mark Twain House

Although Harriet Beecher Stowe and Mark Twain lived as next-door neighbors in Hartford, Connecticut, for nearly two decades, their fame and their literary careers were moving in different directions. When the Stowe family purchased their home at 77 Forest Street in 1873, Stowe was already the most famous woman in America. Her novel *Uncle Tom's Cabin* was the bestselling book of the nineteenth century (besides the Bible) and had propelled the issue of slavery and its abolition into the forefront of America's social and political conscience. Samuel Clemens, on the other hand, was still a rising star writing under the pen name "Mark Twain" when he built an imposing mansion in 1874 at 351 Farmington Avenue. Here, and in his summer residence in Elmira, New York, he wrote the books that gained him national prominence as America's foremost storyteller.

The Stowe and Twain homes are located in Nook Farm, a 140-acre parcel purchased by Stowe's brother-in-law John Hooker and lawyer Francis Gillette in 1853. In the years before and after the Civil War, the neighborhood attracted writers, ministers, politicians, abolitionists, and social reformers who shared Hooker's commitment to social justice and political reform. Many Nook Farm residents were well known and shared a wide range of family, political, and business connections. Hooker's wife, Isabella, was Stowe's half sister and a founder of Connecticut's woman suffrage movement. His partner, Francis Gillette, was a lawyer and abolitionist, whose barn was a stop on the Underground Railroad. Joseph Hawley, publisher of the *Hartford Courant* and later a Civil War general, governor of Connecticut, and U.S. senator, moved with his wife, Harriet, a Beecher cousin, to Nook Farm in 1860. Hawley's friend Charles Warner also lived in Nook Farm and, with Mark Twain, coauthored *The Gilded Age* (1873), a satiric novel about America's newly rich upper class.

Harriet Beecher Stowe and her husband, Calvin, built a Gothic Revival–style home in Nook Farm in 1864 and in 1873 moved to a smaller home that is now the National Historic Landmark the Harriet Beecher Stowe House, where she lived for twenty-two years. In the decade before the Civil War, she had become an international celebrity and one of America's foremost antislavery advocates. She wrote *Uncle Tom's Cabin* in Brunswick, Maine, while her husband taught religion at Bowdoin College. In June 1851, an abolitionist newspaper, *National Era*, began publishing the novel as a forty-one-part series, and John Jewett published the book the next year. Even though it was banned in parts of the South, the book sold 300,000 copies in the United States in less than a year.

Uncle Tom's Cabin riveted readers with its vivid account of the immorality, violence, and tragedy of slavery. Stowe exposed the practice of slave trading, the brutal conditions on many Southern plantations, the dangers of the Underground Railroad, and the tragic consequences of slave hunting as a result of the Fugitive Slave Law of 1850. She created characters that have endured in literary memory—Uncle Tom, the selfless and resourceful slave; Little Eva, the plantation owner's daughter who is saved by Tom's courageous rescue; Eliza and her son, Harry, who narrowly escape to freedom; and the greedy plantation owner Simon Legree.

The impact of *Uncle Tom's Cabin* was worldwide, especially in Great Britain, where more than a dozen editions appeared and where the book inspired songs, games, plays, and commercial products such as soap, scarves, and pottery. At the invitation of antislavery groups in Europe, Stowe journeyed with her family and friends to England, Scotland, France, Italy, and Switzerland. Huge crowds greeted her at every stop and she received many gifts from royalty, various organizations, and admirers, including a twenty-six-volume petition supporting abolition (now displayed at the Stowe Center) signed by more than 560,000 British women.

Stowe maintained an active literary career throughout her life but nothing she wrote equaled the popularity of *Uncle Tom's Cabin.* Her literary reputation would be overshadowed by that of her ambitious and enterprising neighbor, Mark Twain, who moved to Nook Farm with his wife, Olivia, in 1874 with ambitions to establish himself among Hartford's social and cultural elite. They purchased eight acres and commissioned a local architect, Edward Tuckerman Potter, to design a grand Gothic Revival–style mansion with twenty-five rooms and the most modern conveniences of the period. For the interior decoration on the first floor, Twain hired Louis C. Tiffany and Company, who provided lavish scenes inspired by the Middle East and Asia. The Clemens family lived in this house for eighteen years, raising their three daughters and offering hospitality to guests from around the world.

Twain matched the impressive trappings of his home with astounding productivity. He wrote seven books there, including *The Adventures of Tom Sawyer* (1876) and *The Adventures of Huckleberry Finn* (1884). He also launched a book-publishing business and persuaded former president and Civil War hero Ulysses S. Grant to write his memoirs. During this period, Twain achieved the success and fame he dreamed about. He became one of America's bestselling novelists and a popular speaker at dinners and at adult education meetings known as Chautauquas (named for the town in New York where these meetings originated) where he read from his work and offered humorous commentaries on current events.

It is not known whether living next door to Harriet Beecher Stowe inspired him to write *Huckleberry Finn.* It is clear, however, that he shared her concerns about race relations, racism, and the devastating effects of slavery. Through the characters Huck and his slave companion, Jim, Twain wove a series of encounters that represented prevailing racial attitudes before and after the Civil War. The Mississippi River provided the backdrop for the story and became a symbolic character in the novel. Because of its explicit themes and language, including occasional profanity, *Huck Finn* provoked controversy and censorship when it was published and continues to do so today.

By the end of the nineteenth century, the golden age of Nook Farm had ended. Twain's publishing venture failed and he left Nook Farm in 1891. Harriet Beecher Stowe died in 1896, just as the city of Hartford expanded west into the once secluded community of country estates. By the 1950s, many residences became apartments, an interstate highway divided the neighborhood, and the construction of a high school led to the demolition of eleven historic homes. Fortunately, a descendant of the Beecher family, Katharine Seymour Day, saved several Nook Farm homes, including the Stowe and Twain houses. She also arranged for many Beecher family possessions—furnishings, books, art—to return to Hartford as a core collection for the Stowe home. Her extraordinary efforts helped establish the Harriet Beecher Stowe Center and the Mark Twain House & Museum, both places dedicated to preserving and interpreting the life and times of two remarkable Americans and their enduring legacy.

WEBSITES

Harriet Beecher Stowe Center, www.harrietbeecherstowe.org
The Mark Twain House & Museum, www.marktwainhouse.org
Nook Farm, www.connecticuthistory.org/hartfords-nook-farm
Wadsworth Atheneum Museum of Art, www.thewadsworth.org

NEARBY PLACES

Connecticut Historical Society, www.chs.org
Noah Webster House and West Hartford Historical Society,
    www.noahwebsterhouse.org
Connecticut's Old State House, www.cga.ct.gov/osh

26

WILLA CATHER'S GREAT PRAIRIE

RED CLOUD, NEBRASKA

The Willa Cather Memorial Prairie

When she was nine, Willa Cather's family moved to a farm on the prairie near Red Cloud, Nebraska. She left Red Cloud twelve years later, returned often, and stored away enough impressions of life, people, and especially the land to create novels and stories that captured America's frontier experience. With an amazing eye for detail and a magical gift for storytelling, she wrote about the Great Prairie with passion but not with sentimentality. Her books attracted loyal audiences and they are read today by both high school students and scholars. With an original style that blended classical and contemporary themes, she defied trends and movements.

The Cathers came from the Shenandoah Valley community of Back Creek near Winchester, Virginia. During the Civil War this region's strategic importance led to major battles and periods of occupation by both sides. Willa, born in 1873, grew up hearing war stories and witnessed the hard times of the postwar South. Her family began their westward migration in the 1870s to land near Red Cloud between the Republican and Little Blue Rivers known as "the Divide." They were homesteaders, drawn to the prairie by the promise of free land offered by the Homestead Act of 1862. Between 1868 and 1904, Americans from eastern states and immigrants from Scandinavia and Central Europe filed more than 700,000 applications for homesteads. The dream of starting a new life and owning land was compelling, but the harsh reality of surviving on the land overwhelmed many homesteaders, who gave up before completing their commitment to stay five years on the land.

Cather's parents arrived in 1883 but abandoned farming and moved to Red Cloud a year later. After the Burlington and Missouri River

Railroad established a division in town with daily passenger and freight service, Red Cloud's population grew to nearly two thousand. Willa grew up with the town, encouraged by a small group of educated professionals who recognized her precocious talent. Everything about her years in Red Cloud—the train depot, the opera house, the bank, the hardships of farming, the barrenness and beauty of the prairie, the pleasures and pain of small-town life, and especially the triumphs and tragedies of immigrant families—later appeared in her novels, stories, and poetry.

After graduating from the University of Nebraska, she moved to Pittsburgh in 1896, where she edited a monthly magazine, wrote stories, and taught school. In 1906, Samuel McClure, publisher of a New York magazine known for investigative reporting and literary quality, hired her, first as associate editor and later as managing editor, replacing Ida Tarbell, famous for her exposé of the Standard Oil Company. On a research trip to Boston, Cather met popular author Sarah Orne Jewett, who encouraged her to write full-time in her own voice about her experiences. Beginning in 1912, she produced twelve novels and dozens of short stories, creating a rich imaginary world grounded in real places she had lived and visited. Her work earned prizes and praise from her contemporaries. When she died in 1947, the *New York Times* called her "one of the most distinguished of American novelists."

Her prairie trilogy established her reputation as a master of regionalism whose novels chronicled a period that historian Frederick Jackson Turner described in 1893 as "the Closing of the American Frontier." In *O Pioneers!* (1913), she told the story of Alexandra Bergson, a Swedish immigrant who transforms her land into a productive farm. *The Song of the Lark* (1915), considered her most autobiographical work, presented the ambitious Thea Kronborg, also a Swede, as she chases her dream of success as an opera singer. In the final book in the series, *My Ántonia* (1918), a young Czech heroine perseveres through adversity, including the suicide of her father, an attempted rape, and an illegitimate child.

As her characters faced relentless physical, economic, and social pressures, Cather created unforgettable scenes of despair. In *My Ántonia*, a boy recalls the bleakness of the Nebraska prairie: "There seemed to be nothing to see; no fences, no creeks or trees, no hills or fields. . . . There was nothing but land: not a country at all, but the materials out of which countries are made. . . . Between that earth and that sky, I felt erased, blotted out." In the same novel, however, Cather could summon the possibilities of hope and renewal. As Ántonia and her friends watch the sun set, they see the silhouette of a plow against the sun: "Magnified across the distance by the horizontal light, [the plow] . . . was exactly contained within the circle of the disc; the handles, the tongue, the share—black against the molten red. There it was, heroic in size, a picture writing on the sun."

Today, this image is the symbol of the Willa Cather Foundation, which has turned Red Cloud into a living literary monument. Established in 1955 by Mildred Bennett, the foundation now owns five buildings and manages six others for the Nebraska State Historical Society. It provides guided tours, sponsors an annual spring conference, and is building a new museum and archive. The foundation also offers educational programs and hiking trails at a six-hundred-acre tract south of town called the Willa Cather Memorial Prairie, described as a "never-been-plowed prairie ecosystem that preserves plants and wildlife of pre-pioneer days." A hundred miles east of Red Cloud, along Nebraska's Heritage Highway, the Homestead National Monument tells the story of the pioneers and their impact on the land.

No one explored this theme more eloquently than Willa Cather. Her remarkable journey from small-town girl to literary giant is best understood during a tour of the Cather family home in Red Cloud at the corner of Cedar and 3rd Streets, where the family lived from 1884 to 1906. A state highway marker quotes from *The Song of the Lark* and gives Willa Cather the last word: "They turned into another street and saw before them lighted windows; a low story-and-a-half house, with a wing built on at the right and a kitchen addition at the back, everything a little on the slant—roofs, windows, and doors."

COURTESY OF BARB KUDRNA

Willa Cather's Childhood Home

WEBSITES

Willa Cather Foundation, www.willacather.org

Homestead National Monument of America, www.nps.gov/home

NEARBY PLACES

Heritage Highway Byway 136, www.heritagehighway136.com

Starke Round Barn Historic Site, www.starkeroundbarn.com

Captain Meriwether Lewis Dredge and Museum of Missouri River
    History, www.lewisdredge.org

27

INDIAN WARS

LITTLE BIGHORN, MONTANA/WOUNDED KNEE, SOUTH DAKOTA

Little Bighorn Battlefield National Monument

There centuries of conflict in North America between American Indian tribes and European nations came to a violent conclusion on December 29, 1890, in Wounded Knee, South Dakota. On that bitterly cold day, the U.S. Army Seventh Cavalry Regiment, the same regiment defeated at Little Bighorn, Montana, in 1876, massacred nearly three hundred men, women, and children.

The need for land and resources by an expanding American nation overwhelmed legal or traditional claims by Indian tribes. While it is true that many more Indians died from smallpox and other infectious diseases brought by Europeans and that Indians frequently fought and killed each other, the Indian wars that punctuate American history stand out for their consistent pattern of broken treaties, revenge killings, and military conquest. Even nonmilitary events like the Lenape Walking Purchase in Pennsylvania and the Cherokee Trail of Tears from Georgia to Oklahoma are parts of a sad saga of deception, betrayal, and exploitation.

While the outcome of this clash of cultures was inevitable, several remarkable Indian chiefs—King Philip, Pontiac, Cornplanter, Chief Joseph, Tecumseh—arose at various times to lead the resistance against America's relentless expansion. This pantheon also includes Sitting Bull, chief of the Hunkpapa Lakota Sioux and a central figure in the final chapters of the Indian wars.

Born in 1831 in what is now South Dakota, Sitting Bull was a courageous warrior, an excellent hunter, and a charismatic shaman. In his twenties, he fought other Indians and earned the title of warrior chief. His first conflicts with white America began in the early 1860s and accelerated after the Civil War, when Americans turned their attention to securing land in the Great Plains.

In the wars that lasted from 1862 to 1877, the Sioux and other tribes faced a large and formidable army led by experienced Civil War generals, including William T. Sherman and Philip Sheridan. Their goal was to "pacify" the Indians, remove them to reservations, and clear the land for the Northern Pacific Railway and migrants heading west.

The Panic of 1873 stopped construction of the Northern Pacific, but the discovery of gold in South Dakota's Black Hills in 1874 ignited new demands for Indian-occupied lands. Sitting Bull was among the leaders who actively fought this policy, claiming correctly that earlier treaties had given the Indians access to traditional hunting grounds. He rejected military orders to resettle and, in 1876, unified the Sioux, Cheyenne, and other tribes for a major confrontation with federal troops.

By June 1876, more than two thousand U.S. soldiers had assembled in southern Montana, where the Sioux and Cheyenne camped along the Little Bighorn River. On June 22, around four hundred soldiers commanded by Lieutenant Colonel George Custer moved to the south and east of the Indian camp while a larger force waited to attack from the north. Custer, a hero of the Battle of Gettysburg and a veteran of the Great Plains wars, had supreme confidence in his ability to outmaneuver his Indian opponents. He divided his force into three smaller units and ordered an attack on the morning of June 25. However, he had underestimated the size of the Indian force, which outnumbered his regiment by at least three to one.

Custer also underestimated the determination of his opponents. Although Sitting Bull was too old to fight, he had inspired his warriors with a vision of U.S. soldiers being brought "upside down" into their village. The Sioux-Cheyenne alliance easily turned back Custer's assault and launched a deadly counterattack that decimated his regiment. By the morning of June 26, nearly 250 soldiers, including Custer, lay dead.

The Battle of Little Bighorn came a week before Americans planned

TIM BURTON

The Wounded Knee Massacre Monument

to celebrate the centennial of their independence. Custer's defeat dampened the nation's festive mood but also led to a rapid military response. Within a year, Indian resistance had evaporated and Sitting Bull retreated with a small remnant of his tribe into Canada. In 1881, he surrendered and settled in the Standing Rock Reservation.

The Battle of Little Bighorn quickly became part of American folklore. Reenactments of the battle were frequently staged and the Anheuser-Busch beer-brewing company printed thousands of images of "Custer's Last Fight" that hung in bars across the country. Sitting Bull became a celebrity. "Buffalo Bill" Cody invited him to appear in his Wild West Show, where he rode his horse, signed autographs, and befriended Annie Oakley.

The Indian wars, however, were not over. Friction over land ownership continued throughout the 1880s. Furthermore, the reservation system had destroyed traditional Indian culture built on tribal leadership and spiritual values. In 1889, a religious revival—a blend of Indian and Christian beliefs that promised eternal peace free of persecution—swept through the Plains. Followers participated in a ceremony called the Ghost Dance, which stirred great emotional fervor.

The U.S. government saw the Ghost Dance as a new form of resistance and decided to suppress it. Although Sitting Bull was not leading this religion, he supported it and even presided over Ghost Dances at Standing Rock. Reservation officials, fearing Sitting Bull's power to organize resistance, ordered his detention. On December 15, 1890, as police attempted to arrest Sitting Bull, a gun battle broke out that left six police and eight Indians dead, including Sitting Bull. The next day, about 350 Ghost Dancers fled the Standing Rock Reservation and moved south toward Pine Ridge. En route they met the Seventh Cavalry Regiment, which ordered them to assemble at Wounded Knee Creek. As the army attempted to disarm the Indians, a shot went off and the army responded with a barrage of fire. In addition to three hundred Indians, twenty-five soldiers also died, some shot by their own troops.

Little Bighorn Battlefield National Monument is now a popular 765-acre park with guided tours, a national cemetery, and an excellent bookstore. There is, however, no visitor center or bookstore at the monument to the Battle of Wounded Knee. A large historical marker with the word *Massacre* nailed over the word *Battle* provides visitors with the story of the slaughter. A simple iron arch mounted on brick pillars stands at the entrance to a cemetery adjoining a small Catholic church. In 1973, the American Indian Movement occupied this site for seventy-one days to protest living conditions on the Pine Ridge Reservation. Otherwise, the Wounded Knee Monument is an eerily quiet place and its silence obscures the tragedy that happened there.

It is a long drive—seven hours—from Little Bighorn to the Wounded Knee memorial. Along the way, there are two famous sites. The Crazy Horse Memorial, started in 1947 and still under construction, stands nearly six hundred feet high, ten times taller than the other site, the sculpture of four presidents carved into a granite mountain the Sioux call Six Grandfathers. Designed by Gutzon Borglum and completed in 1941, Mount Rushmore is a tribute to great leaders who resolved many national problems. None of them, however, could resolve the conflict between two vastly different civilizations—Indian and white—that defined American history for three hundred years.

WEBSITES

Little Bighorn Battlefield National Monument, www.nps.gov/libi
Red Cloud Indian School, www.redcloudschool.org
Wounded Knee Museum, www.woundedkneemuseum.org

NEARBY PLACES

Mount Rushmore National Memorial, www.nps.gov/moru
Crazy Horse Memorial, www.crazyhorsememorial.org
Buffalo Bill Historical Center, www.codywyomingnet.com/buffalo_bill
    /museum.php

28

THE BRIDGE AND THE STATUE

NEW YORK, NEW YORK

The Brooklyn Bridge

Spectators on the Brooklyn Bridge could barely see the Statue of Liberty through a dense fog and steady rain on the date of its dedication, October 28, 1886. Despite the dreary weather, New York City marked the occasion with a public holiday and the world's first ticker tape parade. Three years earlier, on May 24, 1883, the bridge had opened with an equally joyous event attended by 150,000 people. They marveled at one of the world's greatest engineering feats, a structure compared by many to the Great Pyramid of Egypt that combined innovative, functional design with aesthetic beauty. With the statue in place, New Yorkers could draw further inspiration as their city took shape as a great metropolis.

Both projects had their origins in the decade following the Civil War. New York was a vibrant center of manufacturing, finance, and trade with a population over 800,000 in 1869. Brooklyn, still an independent city, was half the size of New York but growing rapidly. Many Brooklynites commuted by ferry to New York across the East River, but ferry service could be slow and dangerous. A bridge supported by piers in the middle of the river was impractical and difficult to maintain. Only a bridge with a single span high enough to allow river traffic would be appropriate. To design this structure, the New York Bridge Company selected John Roebling, a German-born engineer who had studied philosophy with Friedrich Hegel. His impressive résumé included suspension bridges in Cincinnati, Pittsburgh, and over the Niagara River. He also pioneered in manufacturing wire rope, twisted strands of iron, which he first used at the Allegheny Portage Railroad in western Pennsylvania. He and his sons were operating a profitable wire rope factory in Trenton, New Jersey, when he produced the first drawings of the Brooklyn Bridge. To increase its durability, he specified using steel, first produced in America in 1864, instead of iron for the wire rope. Tragically, he became an early casualty of the project after sustaining an injury that led to his death in 1869. His eldest son, Washington, took over as chief engineer. Trained at Rensselaer Polytechnic Institute and a former Civil War officer, he was able to translate his father's vision into action because of his skills at organizing and managing.

A suspension bridge requires anchorages on each side of a waterway, towers set at intervals in the river itself, cables running from the anchorages over the towers, and a road suspended from the cables. Other suspension bridges already existed in America and around the world. What made the Brooklyn Bridge unique was its magnitude and scale. At 5,989 feet, it was twice as long as any of its contemporaries. Its granite towers, powerful yet as graceful as a medieval cathedral, stood at 276 feet above high water, taller than any building in New York at the time. At their Trenton factory, the Roeblings produced 14,000 miles of wire rope and 1,000 miles of wrapping wire for four tower cables with a total weight of 3,500 tons. In spite of its remarkable stability and strength, Roebling's design also allowed for the road to move as much as two feet as traffic passed over it, a key element in avoiding the structural rigidity that had caused other suspension bridges to collapse.

The most difficult and dangerous challenge in the bridge project was constructing caissons, floating foundations placed into the river's bedrock for the stone towers. Made of heavy wooden timbers, each caisson measured around 170 by 102 feet, weighed more than 3,000 tons, and required seventy-five men to build. Excavating the bedrock for the caissons involved constructing dams to divert the river and a complex ventilating system for men working in 120-foot-deep shafts. This was hazardous, backbreaking work. Injuries were frequent, and on one occasion four men died during the drilling process. The most serious risk of caisson work was contracting "the bends," or caisson disease, a painful and debilitating condition caused by nitrogen bubbles that formed in the blood when a worker moved too quickly from the pressurized caissons to

The Statue of Liberty

the surface. The bridge's official records document more than three hundred cases, including Washington Roebling, who frequently inspected the caissons and spent countless hours in the air locks underground. In 1872, he became sick with the bends and spent much of the next decade confined to his bed in a Brooklyn Heights apartment overlooking the bridge site. His wife, Emily, emerged as a key figure, serving as a major source of communication between Washington and his senior managers. She made vital contributions to the project's successful completion.

Construction of the Statue of Liberty was well under way when the bridge opened. Like many national symbols, such as the flag called "The Star-Spangled Banner" and the Liberty Bell, the original purpose of the statue was quite different from the role it came to play. The idea came from two Frenchmen, Professor Édouard de Laboulaye of Paris, a political philosopher, and Auguste Bartholdi, a sculptor from the Alsace region. They admired America's democratic traditions and applauded the abolition of slavery after the Civil War. Laboulaye proposed a statue to honor America. In 1871, Bartholdi toured the United States to learn about America's national character and to find the best site for the monument he called "Liberty Enlightening the World." He chose New York harbor—the busiest port in the largest city—and identified Bedloe's Island (now called Liberty Island) as the ideal location.

Bartholdi's challenge was to create a statue large enough to be seen from a great distance, like a lighthouse, and sturdy enough to withstand the exposure to the harbor's harsh conditions. He turned for advice to Alexandre Gustave Eiffel, the engineer who later gained fame for the Paris tower that bears his name. Eiffel recommended a skeletal iron framework fastened to a lightweight metal covering. The statue's weight, 225 tons, was supported by the iron frame through a network of beams attached by iron straps to sheets of copper skin. From 1875 to 1884, the statue rose in Bartholdi's Paris workshop to a height of 151 feet. On July 4, 1884, France formally presented the Statue of Liberty to the American people.

The design challenges mirrored the effort to raise $400,000 to build the statue. Laboulaye appealed to donors on both sides of the Atlantic and reached the goal in 1881. Another $125,000 was needed for the statue's 154-foot pedestal, designed by Richard Morris Hunt, the first American trained at the École des Beaux-Arts in Paris. Fund-raising for this project languished even as workers in Paris dismantled the statue, repacked its parts into three hundred crates, and prepared for the ocean voyage to New York. An aggressive campaign by publisher Joseph Pulitzer galvanized public support. It would be, Pulitzer argued, "an irrevocable disgrace to New York City and the American Republic to have

France send us the splendid gift . . . without our having provided even so much as a landing place for it."

In 1883, Pulitzer's newspaper *The World* published a sonnet written by Emma Lazarus, a young poet and activist working to assist Jewish refugees from the pogroms of Czarist Russia. She contributed the sonnet "The New Colossus" to a book auction for the pedestal fund. She called the statue "Mother of Exiles," transforming its meaning with the lines

Give me your tired, your poor,
Your huddled masses yearning to breathe free . . .

For millions of immigrants entering the United States in record numbers the statue was now an icon of freedom. In 1903, long after the 1886 dedication and Lazarus's death in 1887, her poem appeared on a plaque at the statue's base, its powerful message offering "world-wide welcome" to "the homeless, tempest-tost" and the declaration "I lift my lamp beside the golden door."

A new immigration center on nearby Ellis Island became the arrival point for twelve million people between 1892 and 1954. Despite resistance to immigration at various times—the 1920s, 1950s, and 2010s—the role of immigrants in building the United States has been irrefutable. Nearly forty-five million people have immigrated to the United States and a million new immigrants continue to arrive each year. Their presence was dramatically evident on September 11, 2001, when close to three thousand people from 115 countries died in the attacks on the World Trade Center. The National September 11 Memorial & Museum preserves a sacred space and tells the story of victims and survivors, many of whom found safety by crossing the Brooklyn Bridge. On that day, the bridge was a solid source of refuge, and as the smoke and dust cleared from the wreckage at Ground Zero, the statue could be seen still offering hope for a wounded nation's future.

WEBSITES

Statue of Liberty National Monument, www.nps.gov/stli

Brooklyn Bridge, www.nyc.gov/html/dot/html/infrastructure/brooklyn
-bridge.shtml

National September 11 Memorial & Museum, www.911memorial.org

NEARBY PLACES

Lower East Side Tenement Museum, www.tenement.org

Museum of Jewish Heritage, www.mjhnyc.org

Ellis Island, www.nps.gov/elis

African Burial Ground National Monument, www.nps.gov/afbg

29

EDISON'S LABORATORY
WEST ORANGE, NEW JERSEY

Edison's Laboratory

Thomas Edison was—and still is—America's most prolific and most famous inventor. During his lifetime he secured 1,093 patents for everything from the lightbulb to the motion picture camera, and, of equal significance, he built the country's first industrial research and development laboratory. His last and largest complex, located in West Orange, New Jersey, is an impressive landmark of his remarkable career.

He was born in 1847 in Milan, Ohio, and grew up in Port Huron, Michigan. As a young man, he was a telegraph operator fascinated by new electrical technology. At age twenty-two, he decided to become a full-time inventor, and he moved to Newark, New Jersey, in 1870. By 1876, he held around a hundred patents—the first, in 1869, was an electrical vote recorder—and attracted financing for a new laboratory, a frame building that resembled a large barn, in nearby Menlo Park. Edison called it an "Invention Factory," and there he earned the nickname "the Wizard of Menlo Park."

Two Menlo Park inventions—the phonograph and the incandescent lightbulb—offer contrasting examples of his inventive process. The phonograph, patented in 1877, was completely original. Drawing on his understanding of acoustics, Edison and his assistants worked for months on a machine that could reproduce the human voice. Edison called his unique device "the apparatus" and his staff tried at least twenty names, among them telautograph, polyphone, autophone, hulagmophone, and glottophone, before settling on phonograph, a talking machine.

The lightbulb, on the other hand, was not new. Throughout the nineteenth century, scientists in France and England had publicly displayed battery-powered lighting, and in America, electric lights were used in lighthouses and streetlamps. To make a light practical for everyday use, however, required a way to control its intensity. In 1879, Edison announced the discovery that a material made of carbon could serve as a conductor, or filament, for electric light and burn in a glass-enclosed vacuum—a lightbulb—powered by an electric generator. Three years later, Edison opened the world's first central power station on Pearl Street in lower Manhattan. During the 1880s, the Edison Electric Light Company built power stations in several Northeast cities. In 1890, Edison established the Edison General Electric Company, and in 1892, it merged with a competitor, the Thomson-Houston Electric Company, to form General Electric, one of America's most successful and innovative companies.

With the exception of his light and power system, Edison was more engaged in producing and licensing his inventions than in manufacturing and marketing the products he developed. The laboratory complex in West Orange, completed in 1888, represented his commitment to research and development. The main building is an enormous three-story brick structure with a library, machine shop, laboratory, and Edison's office. Labs for chemistry, physics, and metallurgy are nearby. The most distinctive building, built in 1893 and called Black Maria, was the world's first motion picture studio, featuring a revolving building with a hinged roof to allow use of direct sunlight. Here, Edison and his staff filmed ballet performances and boxing matches, and made educational films. In 1902, he filmed the first demonstration of yoga.

The West Orange laboratory produced some of Edison's most successful inventions, including more reliable models of the phonograph, the motion picture camera and projector, cement manufacturing technology, and the alkaline storage battery. Originally designed for electric automobiles, the battery became widely used in many industrial applications.

Although Edison's accomplishments brought international acclaim, he did experience some notable, and costly, failures. During the 1890s, for example, he tried to develop an electromagnetic ore separator to produce iron briquettes for steel mills. He purchased a mine in northern New Jersey and lived there for five years. He invested more than $2 million in a massive complex to mine, crush, separate, and concentrate iron ore. However, the discovery of iron deposits in Minnesota's Mesabi Range drove down iron prices and forced Edison to abandon his enterprise. "Well, it's all gone," he lamented, "but we had a good time spending it."

Edison maintained an intense and sometimes very public competition with notable rivals. He outpaced Alexander Graham Bell, inventor of the telephone, to create the phonograph. In the 1880s, his "War of the Currents" with George Westinghouse attracted widespread attention. Westinghouse, a Pittsburgh industrialist and inventor of the locomotive air brake, had adopted alternating current, a form of electric transmission to deliver power and light inexpensively through overhead wires. Edison favored direct current, a more expensive and less flexible approach, fed through conduits buried underground. Edison believed, correctly, that alternating current was dangerous and, as a way to discredit Westinghouse, promoted its use in capital punishment. In 1890, New York became the first state to employ the electric chair and used alternating current to carry out the death sentence. However, the public accepted the safety risk in exchange for the cheaper power and light. Westinghouse and alternating current prevailed.

At the West Orange laboratory, a loyal and dedicated staff of engineers and scientists demonstrated the value of collective enterprise in the invention process. Edison's intelligence, prodigious work ethic, and unique brand of leadership created the environment that encouraged innovation. The accomplishments of this laboratory overshadowed all the defeats and frustrations. Today, the National Park Service manages the original complex, including a 1950s replica of the movie studio as well as Edison's home, Glenmont, an imposing twenty-nine-room house built in the 1880s, located nearby.

No one was more loyal or admiring of Edison than Henry Ford, who had worked briefly for an Edison company before becoming America's foremost automobile manufacturer. They later became good friends and drew national attention, beginning in 1918 with a series of well-publicized camping trips. To celebrate the fiftieth anniversary of Edison's electric light in 1929, Ford arranged for a special ceremony at Greenfield Village, his new museum near Detroit, and re-created the Menlo Park laboratory as a permanent exhibition.

When Edison died in 1931, President Herbert Hoover asked Americans to pay tribute by turning off their electric lights at 10 p.m. Eastern time. He also considered shutting down the nation's generators but realized how much America depended on electricity. A world powered by electricity, and created, in many respects, by Thomas Edison, could not stand still.

WEBSITES

Thomas Edison National Historical Park, www.nps.gov/edis
The Thomas Edison Center at Menlo Park, www.menloparkmuseum.org

NEARBY PLACES

The Thomas Edison Papers, edison.rutgers.edu
Grover Cleveland Birthplace, www.presidentcleveland.org

30

WORLD'S COLUMBIAN EXPOSITION

CHICAGO, ILLINOIS

Museum of Science and Industry

"Make no little plans; they have no magic to stir men's blood," said Daniel Burnham, director of the World's Columbian Exposition. His words reflect the ambitious and unprecedented Chicago fair that captivated America and the world in 1893. Organized to celebrate the four hundredth anniversary of the voyages of Christopher Columbus, the exposition became a symbol of progress in technology, architecture, landscape design, and urban planning. It ran only six months but attracted more attention and achieved greater influence than any similar event in America before or since.

Burnham was a successful architect and urban planner who, with his partner, John Wellborn Root, designed some of Chicago's major commercial buildings after the Great Chicago Fire of 1871. They promoted the city's winning bid to host the fair and Burnham signed on as director of works. To design the 630-acre campus, he assembled the nation's greatest architects—Richard Morris Hunt, Charles F. McKim, Louis Sullivan—and oversaw construction of two hundred buildings in less than three years. Frederick Law Olmsted, America's leading landscape architect, created the park; Sophie Hayden, one of America's first female architects, designed the Women's Building; and sculptor Augustus Saint-Gaudens served as an artistic advisor. The total construction cost was $28 million.

Nearly 27.5 million people paid fifty cents each to visit the fair. They experienced an extraordinary display dominated by enormous neoclassical buildings—the Court of Honor—surrounding a reflecting pool. This architectural assemblage became known as the "White City"—an urban fantasy that stood in stark contrast to the mostly unpleasant conditions of Chicago and other American cities. As visitors strolled through Olmsted's beautiful park on the edge of Lake Michigan, they visited pavilions representing forty-six nations and major industries such as manufacturing, transportation, electricity, and agriculture.

The Midway Plaisance, a mile-long amusement park, featured food, music, rides, a traveling zoo, a reproduction of an Irish castle, a Javanese village, and dancing girls from Cairo. The highlight of the Midway was the world's first Ferris wheel, designed by Pittsburgh engineer George Ferris; the 250-foot steel ride could carry two thousand people at a time.

The Hindu monk Vivekananda, a founder of the modern yoga renaissance, introduced Hindu philosophy at the Parliament of Religions, the largest of many congresses held during the exposition and the first formal international interfaith dialogue. At the annual meeting of the American Historical Association, Frederick Jackson Turner delivered his presidential address on "The Closing of the American Frontier." He argued that the frontier—the unsettled and undeveloped lands of the West—had a profound effect on American society and its democratic traditions. By the 1890s, America was no longer a frontier society, and this reality would alter its national identity in the future.

Yet as Turner proclaimed the end of the frontier, one of the most popular attractions on a fifteen-acre site just outside the fairgrounds was "Buffalo Bill's Wild West and Congress of Rough Riders of the World." More than four million people flocked to a show that included historical and wildlife displays; encampments of Indians, soldiers, and workers; and gun collections. An 18,000-seat arena featured a spectacular show that included a Grand Review of soldiers from six countries, marksmanship by Annie Oakley, and reenactments of the Battle of Little Bighorn. Cody left Chicago with a $1 million profit that he used to found the town of Cody, Wyoming.

Like Cody's Wild West show, the White City flourished. Future presidents—Theodore Roosevelt and Woodrow Wilson—were guests. Harry Houdini, Thomas Edison, Susan B. Anthony, and Eadweard Muybridge visited. An entrepreneur from Pennsylvania, Milton Hershey, watched a demonstration of German machinery for producing milk chocolate and returned home with a plan for making candy.

L. Frank Baum, a traveling salesman and aspiring writer, wandered through the fair transfixed by the spectacle of the dreamlike architecture decorated with sculptures of mythological and historical figures, the Midway with the Ferris wheel, the tethered hot-air balloon, and the Electricity Building's futuristic gadgets and flashing Tower of Light. The fair glimmered with electricity; a giant rotating spotlight was visible from a hundred miles away at night. Baum's frequent visits shaped *The Wonderful Wizard of Oz*, his 1900 children's book that inspired the classic 1939 movie.

While the fair prospered, the grim reality of local and national events challenged its progressive image. An economic crisis triggered by bank failures and the collapse of railroad stocks spread through the country. South of the White City, a conflict between rail car manufacturer George Pullman and workers in what had been a "model industrial town" turned into a major strike in May 1894 that required the intervention of federal troops.

Thousands of homeless and unemployed people, displaced by the worsening depression, descended on Chicago and, after the fair closed, occupied the same grounds where visitors had celebrated the wonders of the exposition. Arsonists set fire to major exposition buildings and the flames that rose over Lake Michigan replaced the spectacular display of electric lights in the night sky.

Only one building—the Palace of Fine Arts—survived from the World's Columbian Exposition. In the 1920s, Julius Rosenwald, former chairman of Sears, Roebuck and Company, led a campaign to renovate the building and create the Museum of Science and Industry that today offers a rich variety of exhibitions and learning experiences. Jackson Park and the Midway Plaisance also survived, reminders of the fair's lasting impact on Chicago as a center of architecture and urban planning. The legacy of the fair also gave rise to a national City Beautiful movement, which inspired new thinking about the potential of cities and technology at the dawn of the twentieth century.

WEBSITE

Museum of Science and Industry, www.msichicago.org

NEARBY PLACES

Chicago History Museum, www.chicagohistory.org

Historic Pullman Foundation, www.pullmanil.org

Adler Planetarium, www.adlerplanetarium.org

Jane Addams Hull-House Museum, www.hullhousemuseum.org

31

BILTMORE HOUSE

ASHEVILLE, NORTH CAROLINA

Biltmore House

As George Washington Vanderbilt II's palatial estate rose on a mountaintop overlooking the French Broad River, it instantly became a monument to an era—named "the Gilded Age" by Mark Twain—of fabulous wealth and ostentatious display. More than any single residence in the country, Biltmore House reflected the success and tastes of America's elite class, what social critic Thorstein Veblen called "conspicuous consumption." It also reflected its patron's expansive vision, and was far more ambitious than anything being built by his contemporaries in Manhattan, along the Hudson River, at Newport, Rhode Island, or on Philadelphia's Main Line.

Vanderbilt was the grandson of Cornelius Vanderbilt, America's wealthiest man in the nineteenth century. At the time of his death in 1877, Cornelius Vanderbilt left an estate valued at $100 million, and by 1889 the wealth of the Vanderbilt family totaled around $300 million ($7.5 billion in 2010 dollars).

George Vanderbilt was not involved in family businesses. Instead, he spent his inheritance traveling the world, collecting books and art, and building what is still one of America's largest private dwellings. His selection of a site in North Carolina, far from the wealthy enclaves of the Northeast, came at a time when the South, especially the southern Appalachians, was still recovering from the economic devastation of the Civil War. Biltmore represented a significant change for the region, a rare example of a major financial investment by a Northerner.

Vanderbilt recruited the nation's most prominent designers to create his estate. Richard Morris Hunt, whose work included Vanderbilt family mansions in New York and Newport, served as senior architect. To design the gardens and park surrounding the mansion, Hunt recruited his friend Frederick Law Olmsted, designer of New York's Central Park and considered the founding father of landscape architecture in America. From 1889 to 1895, they hired artists, craftsmen, stonemasons, horticulturists, and other specialists along with hundreds of workers who built the mansion and gardens and laid out the farms and woodlands. The massive undertaking required a private railroad to transport supplies, and factories for brickmaking and woodworking.

On Christmas Eve 1895, George Vanderbilt opened Biltmore House to family and friends. What they saw was the most extraordinary house in the country. Olmsted's three-mile Approach Road created a dramatic entry. Guests arrived at a mansion with a 375-foot-wide façade inspired by the châteaux of France's Loire Valley. As they wandered through the main floor, they encountered rooms that showcased outstanding craftsmanship and displayed a magnificent collection of art, sculpture, prints, books, and furnishings.

Vanderbilt entertained in a banquet hall with sixteenth-century Flemish tapestries, a triple fireplace with an overmantel carved by Karl Bitter, and an oak dining table with two built-in throne chairs and enough room for 67 dinner guests. He often invited his guests to a library that contained 10,000 books—less than half his overall collection—and a ceiling painting he purchased from a Venetian palace ballroom. The 250-room house covers nearly four acres, including 33 bedrooms, 43 bathrooms, 65 fireplaces, three kitchens, an indoor swimming pool, a bowling alley, and modern conveniences such as elevators and refrigerators. Outside the mansion, Olmsted designed a 250-acre park that he considered his finest work. A 75-acre walled garden, inspired by English manor houses, included open-air themed "rooms" such as the Azalea Garden and the Rose Garden.

Three elements at Vanderbilt's estate reflected the progressive ideals that set it apart from other grand estates of its time: a school of forestry, a planned community, and a self-sustaining farm and workshop. He hired a young conservationist, Gifford Pinchot, to manage the 125,000-acre forest that covered his mountaintop estate. Pinchot had attended the French National School of Forestry and introduced the practice of controlled timbering at Biltmore, making the estate the first managed forest in the country and recognized as "the cradle of American forestry." Pinchot later served as first chief of the U.S. Forest Service and was elected twice as governor of Pennsylvania.

Vanderbilt also commissioned Hunt and Olmsted to design Biltmore Village, a planned community of shops and houses anchored by a school, an infirmary, a train station, and the Cathedral of All Souls (Episcopal), an architectural hybrid of Romanesque and Gothic styles. Construction of the village began in 1897 and the first residents occupied their homes in 1900. At Vanderbilt's request, Hunt designed the Young Men's Institute, a recreation center for African Americans located in downtown Asheville, now a cultural center.

In 1897, Vanderbilt established Biltmore Farms, one of the largest dairies in the Southeast, and in 1901 he founded Biltmore Industries, famous for its textile products. These businesses employed local workers and provided revenue for the estate's operations. Vanderbilt's wife, Edith Stuyvesant Dresser, whom he married in 1898, took a special interest in the production of woven fabrics and quilts, and supported a school to train local women in these crafts. She also played a pivotal role in sustaining and preserving Biltmore House. For fifteen years, she served as hostess of the mansion and supervised an enormous household staff. After George died in 1914, she ensured Biltmore's survival by selling 87,000 acres of forest to the federal government, which became the nucleus of Pisgah National Forest. She also sold Biltmore Industries and Biltmore Village. Her daughter, Cornelia, and her husband, John Cecil, opened Biltmore to the public in 1930 and their sons, William and George, continued the family tradition of maintaining the estate as a self-supporting business. Today, more than one million people each year visit an 8,000-acre park that offers recreation, a winery, an inn, restaurants, shops, and tours of the incomparable house and gardens of Biltmore.

WEBSITE
Biltmore Estate, www.biltmore.com

NEARBY PLACES
Historic Biltmore Village, www.biltmorevillage.com
Biltmore Industries, Inc., www.nps.gov/nr/travel/asheville/ind.htm
Grovewood Gallery, www.grovewood.com
Cradle of Forestry, www.cradleofforestry.com/site
Thomas Wolfe Memorial State Historic Site, www.wolfememorial.com
Young Men's Institute Building/YMI Cultural Center of Asheville,
    www.nps.gov/nr/travel/asheville/you.htm or
    www.ymiculturalcenter.org

32

TALIESIN
SPRING GREEN, WISCONSIN

Taliesin

Late in his life, Frank Lloyd Wright was testifying in a legal proceeding. Asked to state his profession, he said, "I'm the world's greatest architect." After the hearing, his wife advised that he should try to be more modest. "But remember," he responded, "I was under oath!" Wright could back up his boasts. He was the most innovative and influential architect in American history, and he remains the standard by which architects and architecture in this country are measured.

Taliesin is the starting point for understanding Wright's life and work. Located in Wisconsin's Wyoming Valley about forty miles west of Madison, the house and the surrounding landscape reflect his philosophy, ambition, and achievements. Taliesin was also the setting for personal crises and one extraordinary tragedy.

Wright built Taliesin near his birthplace, Richland Center, a small community of Welsh farmers. He grew up listening to sermons by Unitarian preachers and reading Ralph Waldo Emerson and other transcendentalists, whose philosophy shaped his commitment to individualism and experimentation. His mother always wanted him to be an architect and gave him gifts—wooden blocks, pegs, and colored paper—designed by the German educator Friedrich Froebel. Wright later acknowledged the influence of these toys on his architecture.

A below-average student with a great talent for drawing, Wright dropped out of college, moved to Chicago, and enjoyed a brief but productive collaboration with Louis Sullivan, the leading designer of skyscrapers and other commercial buildings. Wright always recognized his intellectual debt to Sullivan, whom he called *Lieber Meister* (Dear Master).

In 1893, Wright started his own firm, moved to Oak Park, a Chicago suburb, and designed buildings that established his reputation as a genius, an American original. Borrowing ideas from contemporary European architecture and traditional Japanese design, he invented the Prairie style. Wright's houses, in his words, "broke the box" of the traditional symmetrical vertical house forms. His houses were horizontal structures with bands of windows under low roofs. He opened up interiors by creating a single space for dining and entertaining anchored by a fireplace at the center. He also connected the building with its natural setting through plazas and terraces, creating what he called "organic architecture."

Within a few years after moving to Oak Park, Frank Lloyd Wright was at the top of his profession, recognized as the most original and promising architect of the new century. Then, in 1909, he walked away from his practice and left his wife and six children. A love affair with Mamah Borthwick Cheney, the wife of a client, became a public scandal that forced him to leave America on a self-imposed exile to Europe. The need to escape the scrutiny of the media and ensure his privacy led Wright to plan Taliesin on his family's land in rural Wisconsin.

Inspired by the landscape of his youth and by his love for Borthwick (now divorced), Wright envisioned Taliesin as a home in complete harmony with nature. In Welsh, *taliesin* means "shining brow," and he chose the name to show respect for the land. In his autobiography, he wrote, "This hill on which Taliesin now stands as a 'brow' was one of my favorite places when I was a boy. . . . And it was unthinkable that any house should be put on that beloved hill. I knew well by now that no house should ever be on any hill or on anything. It should be of the hill, belonging to it, so hill and house could live together each the happier for the other." The siting of the house, the orientation of the entrance and windows, the arrangement of porches and plazas all reflected Wright's commitment to organic architecture. He used local materials to reinforce this vision. Other buildings on the estate—farm buildings, a residence for his sister, a school—also conformed to these principles.

Wright and Borthwick moved into Taliesin in 1911 and his architectural practice rebounded. The tranquility of their rural retreat ended shockingly, however, on August 15, 1914, when a house servant, Julian Carleton, set fire to Taliesin's living quarters and then attacked Borthwick, her two children, and several workers with an ax as they tried to escape. By the end of Carleton's inexplicable and insane rampage, seven people were dead, including Borthwick and the children.

The violence of that day shattered Wright forever. He recovered only by devoting himself to his work and rebuilding Taliesin. While he enjoyed professional success as an architect, his private life remained turbulent with love affairs, divorces, client lawsuits, financial woes, and endless media attention. To add to his troubles, an electrical fire in 1925 destroyed much of Taliesin. But once again, Wright rebuilt the house and renamed it Taliesin III, his home and studio for the rest of his life.

In the 1930s, Wright revived his career and entered a period of astonishing productivity. In 1932, he published his autobiography and another book, *The Disappearing City*, in which he presented a utopian vision based on decentralized rural communities comprised of single-family homes. Wright called his proposal "Broadacre City," rejecting high-density urban centers and relying on automobiles for transportation. He designed a low-cost house, the Usonian home, a simple but functional response to contemporary needs. Although Broadacre City never gained popularity, Wright built more than a hundred Usonian homes for middle-income clients.

To sustain his practice during the Great Depression, Wright founded the Taliesin Fellowship in 1932, bringing men and women to live and work communally at Taliesin. Under Wright's tutelage, the Fellowship grew into a loyal cadre of architects committed to his philosophy. The Fellowship continues today at both Taliesin and Taliesin West, a winter home and studio Wright built in Scottsdale, Arizona, in 1937. One of his students at Taliesin, Edgar Kaufmann Jr., introduced Wright to his father, owner of Pittsburgh's largest department store, who retained Wright to design a country retreat on Bear Run, a stream in western

Pennsylvania. The home, called Fallingwater (1938), is Wright's master-piece, named the "Best Building of the 20th Century" by the American Institute of Architects.

Before his death in 1959, Wright established the Frank Lloyd Wright Foundation, which owns and manages an archival collection and Wright's estates in Wisconsin and Arizona. Taliesin Preservation, Inc. (TPI), founded in 1991, manages the six-hundred-acre Taliesin site and preserves several historic structures, including the estate and Hillside, a school Wright designed for his aunts that later served as his studio and home for the Taliesin Fellowship. Throughout the year, TPI offers programs and tours that sustain the legacy of an artist who, despite the disharmony of his life, produced a harmonious vision of architecture and the land.

WEBSITE
Taliesin, www.taliesinpreservation.org

NEARBY PLACES
Frank Lloyd Wright Foundation/Taliesin West, www.franklloydwright
    .org/about/TaliesinWestTours.html
Wright in Wisconsin, www.wrightinwisconsin.org

33

FIRST FLIGHT
KILL DEVIL HILLS, NORTH CAROLINA

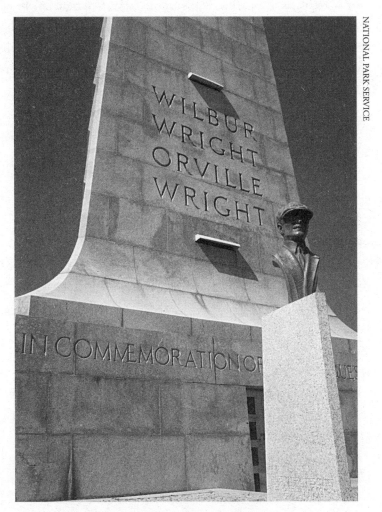

Wright Brothers National Memorial

To determine who would be the first to pilot their flying machine, the Wright brothers flipped a coin. Wilbur won but he tried to elevate the plane too quickly and crashed into a sand dune. Three days later— December 17, 1903—his younger brother, Orville, took the controls and for twelve seconds flew the world's first controlled, powered aircraft. They tested their new invention—605 pounds of wire, wood, cloth, and a four-cylinder engine producing 12 horsepower—three more times that day. On the fourth try, Wilbur had his turn and, flying into a 27 mph wind, stayed aloft for almost one minute. The Age of Flight had begun.

The brothers were self-taught mechanics who built, maintained, and sold bicycles in a shop they opened in 1892 in Dayton, Ohio. Neither man pursued a college education, but their obsession with flying drove them to absorb as much information as they could on the subject. They observed birds and the movements of kites. They corresponded with the Smithsonian Institution on aeronautical research and consulted with the National Weather Service to find the best site for flying. In a homemade wind tunnel, they tested more than two hundred wing shapes. Like countless American inventors before them and thousands more who followed, they worked in obscurity, self-financed, driven by a passion to apply scientific principles to solve technological problems.

The Wrights had to solve three technical challenges: thrust, lift, and control. The plane's engine and propellers provided thrust to move forward; the wing design allowed for lift to raise the plane off the ground; and movable parts—ailerons, or flaps on the wings, and a rudder and elevator on the tail, enabled a pilot to control the plane. The Wrights' method of flight control, patented in 1906, was their most important achievement. Today, it remains the basic element in airplane design.

The Outer Banks of North Carolina offered the best flying conditions—free of obstructions, with steady winds, high ground to launch their machine, and soft ground for landing. Beginning in 1900, the brothers made four annual visits to the area, and in 1901 selected Kill Devil Hills, a series of dunes four miles south of Kitty Hawk, to conduct manned and unmanned flights with gliders. The Kitty Hawk community welcomed their Ohio visitors and formed a special bond with the Wrights as they pursued their dream. U.S. Coast Guard captain William Tate befriended the brothers, and a member of the Kitty Hawk Life Saving Station, John T. Daniels, played the key role of operating the camera that produced images of the historic flights on that cold December day.

For the next few years, the Wrights continued to work on airplane design, returning to Kitty Hawk twice, then demonstrating a new plane in France, where they were hailed as heroes. They formed companies to manufacture planes in France, Germany, and America, and in 1908 they secured a U.S. government contract. In 1909, they completed a successful twenty-mile flight over New York City as a million spectators watched. After Wilbur's death in 1912, Orville continued the business until 1915.

Although Europeans generally recognized their pioneering efforts, the Wrights faced controversy at home. They spent years in litigation with rivals, especially Glenn Curtiss, over patent rights. Another conflict was with the Smithsonian Institution, whose secretary, Samuel Langley, had attempted to become the first person to fly. Although his efforts were unsuccessful, the Smithsonian still refused to recognize the Wright brothers as the first to fly and claimed that a version of Langley's plane modified by Curtiss proved that it was the first plane "capable of sustained free flight." In protest, Orville Wright reconstructed the original Wright Flyer and placed it on loan in 1928 to the London Science Museum. The Smithsonian finally reversed its position in 1942, and Orville agreed to return the Flyer to the United States. The Smithsonian's National Air and Space Museum in Washington now displays the Wright Flyer in a special gallery and acknowledges the Wright brothers' singular achievement.

The Wright Brothers National Memorial near Kitty Hawk commemorates the achievement of the first flights. Dedicated in 1932, the sixty-foot-tall granite tower stands on a ninety-foot sand dune and honors the inventors with the word *genius* carved at its base. A trail marking the four 1903 flights runs past a visitor center built in 1960 as part of the National Park Service's Mission 66 program. Designed by the Philadelphia firm Mitchell/Giurgola Architects, the center displays replicas of the 1902 glider and the 1903 flyer along with original tools, machines, and other artifacts. A Centennial of Flight Pavilion opened in 2003 with more exhibits and programs.

The significance of the Outer Banks is not limited to the history of flight. About fourteen miles from Kitty Hawk is Fort Raleigh, where the first English settlers established a village on Roanoke Island in 1584. Every summer, a historical drama, *The Lost Colony*, tells the story of the community that mysteriously disappeared after six years. Within an hour's drive of Roanoke Island are landmarks of navigation and maritime history—the Chicamacomico Life Saving Station (1874) and Cape Hatteras Lighthouse (1870). The Graveyard of the Atlantic Museum, opened in 2002 near the lighthouse, documents the history of shipwrecks, including the USS *Monitor*, the Civil War ironclad that sank in December 1862.

A visit to the Outer Banks should also include Nags Head, nine miles south of Kitty Hawk and the home of Jockey's Ridge State Park, a series of sand dunes and a spectacular setting for hang gliding. Nearby, beach cottages built in the late nineteenth and early twentieth centuries, popularly known as the "unpainted aristocracy," evoke a time when two brothers from Ohio turned a remote stretch of barrier islands into the birthplace of modern aviation.

WEBSITES
Wright Brothers National Memorial, www.nps.gov/wrbr
Wright Brothers Aeroplane Company, www.wright-brothers.org

NEARBY PLACES
The Outer Banks, www.outerbanks.org
Cape Hatteras Light Station, www.nps.gov/caha/planyourvisit/chls.htm
Fort Raleigh National Historic Site, www.nps.gov/fora
Chicamacomico Life Saving Station Historic Site & Museum,
    www.chicamacomico.net/
Graveyard of the Atlantic Museum, www.graveyardoftheatlantic.com

34

GRAND CENTRAL TERMINAL

NEW YORK, NEW YORK

The Grand Central Terminal Clock

Above the south entrance to Grand Central Terminal stands a bronze statue of Cornelius Vanderbilt. It is appropriately larger than life, twelve feet tall. More than any individual, Vanderbilt shaped the development of New York in the nineteenth century. The statue's location is also appropriate; more than any other building, Grand Central Terminal transformed the city's development in the twentieth century.

In the nineteenth century, two buildings called Grand Central, a depot and later a station, occupied the site at Forty-Second Street and Fourth Avenue. The depot (1871) served three rail lines Vanderbilt consolidated as the New York Central and Hudson River Railroad. He had started out in the ferry and steamship business, earning the nickname "Commodore," eventually amassing a fortune valued at $100 million at the time of his death in 1877. His son William doubled this fortune. Contemporary critics labeled the Vanderbilts "robber barons" who amassed enormous wealth and power through the ruthless defeat of competitors, the corruption of government officials, and the exploitation of workers. Later historians were more charitable, citing the Vanderbilts' remarkable business acumen and their contributions to economic growth.

The Vanderbilts' dominance in New York gradually declined, but the company they created grew in importance. In 1898, New York Central enlarged the depot into an impressive station that served sixteen million passengers annually. By that time, however, the city's population had expanded north of Forty-Second Street and steam locomotives transiting Park Avenue at street level made life noisy, congested, and dangerous. In the 1880s, the company lowered portions of the tracks and constructed bridges across them for local traffic. Residents were safer but passengers on trains endured dark, hot, and smoky conditions. Conductors could barely see hazards that might lie ahead of them. Fears of an accident became reality on January 8, 1902, when train 118 from White Plains ran into a parked commuter train, killing seventeen passengers and injuring thirty-four.

The crash prompted state legislation that banned steam locomotives from the city no later than 1908. At the same time, the Pennsylvania Railroad announced a plan to tunnel under the Hudson River and build a new station on the city's west side. Challenged by the new law and competition from its archrival, New York Central responded with a bold plan, devised by chief engineer William Wilgus, to power trains by electricity and construct an underground two-level platform to serve long-distance and suburban passengers, and turning loops to avoid delays. A majestic new terminal, the world's largest, would anchor the entire complex. His most ingenious idea was to cover the rail yards and tracks from the terminal north to Fifty-Sixth Street, and sell the rights to develop the forty-eight-acre parcel along this new wide boulevard. The sale of "air rights" (a term that Wilgus coined in 1903) to twenty-five aboveground parcels provided revenue to pay for the electrification project and made Park Avenue the city's most desirable address. To link both sections of Park Avenue, Wilgus also proposed a roadway around the terminal.

New York Central invested the 2013 equivalent of $2 billion in the Wilgus plan. Using direct-current technology developed by Thomas Edison and Frank Sprague, it completed the electrification initiative in 1906. The terminal construction project took ten years and employed 10,000 workers, who removed more than three million cubic yards of dirt and debris to create train tunnels, an electrical substation, a water heating plant, a traffic control tower, and a drainage sewer that carried water through six-foot-diameter pipes a half mile to the East River.

To design the terminal, the railroad first selected Reed and Stem from St. Paul, Minnesota, then added the New York firm Warren and Wetmore, forming an association fraught with conflict but somehow capable of producing a landmark of Beaux Arts architecture. They engaged

The Grand Central Terminal Concourse

several Parisian artists, including Sylvain Salières, who designed the decorative details; Jules-Félix Coutan, who designed *Transportation*, the enormous sculpture above Forty-Second Street with the figures of Mercury, Hercules, and Minerva representing travel, strength, and wisdom, respectively; and Paul César Helleu, who conceived the sky-blue mural on the main concourse ceiling with the constellations of the October sky from Aquarius to Cancer. The 38,000-square-foot concourse served as a magnificent gateway to the city.

Grand Central was an aesthetic spectacle but also a place that catered to the comforts and needs of passengers with pedestrian ramps, a central information booth, restaurants such as the Oyster Bar, jewelry and clothing stores, newsstands, and flower and cigar shops. Underground walkways connected passengers to offices, stores, hotels, and residences. For many passengers, a unique experience was walking the red carpet as they boarded the *20th Century Limited* bound for Chicago. In 1923, an art gallery opened, selling paintings and sculptures by major artists, and an art school started operations the next year. In the late 1930s, the

Columbia Broadcasting System built its first television studio above the main waiting room.

Wilgus and his architects had a bold vision that encompassed the terminal's surrounding neighborhood. Inspired by the City Beautiful movement that encouraged planning and beautification, they proposed Terminal City, an integrated thirty-two-block city within a city that eventually included the Commodore and Waldorf-Astoria hotels, the Chrysler Building, and the New York Central (now Helmsley) Building. Although the plan was not fully realized, it shaped midtown Manhattan's development from Times Square and Rockefeller Center to the United Nations headquarters at the East River.

Following World War II, travel by cars and planes caused a dramatic decline in passenger rail. Grand Central Terminal symbolized this change. The New York Central Railroad desperately tried to generate revenue by leasing the concourse for advertising and subdividing its commercial space. The building deteriorated; the roof leaked and the blue ceiling mural turned black with tobacco smoke. The art gallery and television studio relocated. In time, hundreds of homeless people occupied the waiting rooms overnight. The era of the red carpet treatment was over.

In the 1950s, the railroad tried to develop its real estate around the terminal. It allowed construction of a fifty-nine-story building that dwarfed the terminal and, after merging with the Pennsylvania Railroad in 1968, planned another fifty-five-story skyscraper over the terminal itself, threatening its structural and architectural integrity. That proposal sparked a preservation campaign by a coalition that included former First Lady Jacqueline Kennedy Onassis. "Is it not cruel to let our city die by degrees," she wrote in 1975, "stripped of all her proud moments, until there will be nothing left of all her history and beauty to inspire our children? If they are not inspired by the past of our city, where will they find the strength to fight for her future?" In 1978, after a decade of debate and litigation, the U.S. Supreme Court upheld New York City's Landmarks Law, which provided for the protection of historic buildings, the first time it had ruled in a historic preservation case.

The fight to save the terminal also generated a new commitment to restore its former glory. Metro-North, the public agency managing commuter rail service, and its president, Peter Stangl, spearheaded this effort, investing in basic repairs and engaging architect John Belle to prepare a master plan that generated more than $800 million in public investment, including restoration of the concourse's ceiling mural. Private development gradually returned. Grand Central Terminal now serves millions of commuters and is a magnet for tourists, who can take guided tours or simply wander through one of urban America's defining achievements.

WEBSITE
Grand Central Terminal, www.gcthistory.com

NEARBY PLACES
Rockefeller Center, www.rockefellercenter.com
Times Square, www.timessquarenyc.org/visitor-tips/history/index
    .aspx#.U_KKmvldWSo
United Nations, www.un.org

35

BIRTHPLACE OF JAZZ

NEW ORLEANS, LOUISIANA

Louis Armstrong Park

On New Year's Eve in 1912, a poor eleven-year-old African American boy named Louis Armstrong was arrested for firing a pistol near his home in New Orleans's Third Ward. As punishment he spent eighteen months at the Colored Waifs' Home, where he learned to play popular songs on a cornet. When he came home, he began playing jazz, the new music sweeping the urban South, and launched a storybook career as a musician, entertainer, and cultural ambassador.

New Orleans was the perfect setting to nurture the talent and ambition of Louis Armstrong. Founded by the French in 1718, it was an international seaport attracting people from around the world who brought with them the music of their homeland. Dancing was also integral to the city's cultural life—including ballroom dances such as the waltz, polka, mazurka, and schottische—as were marching bands and parades, and weekly gatherings in Congo Square staged by the city's large slave population. New Orleans residents attended musical performances of all kinds, from opera and chamber music to the elaborate processions of Mardi Gras to informal gatherings in parks and at festivals. After the Civil War, the audience for music in New Orleans increased to include thousands of black migrants, including Armstrong's family, from plantations in the Mississippi delta.

The late nineteenth century was a time when the rigid code of racial segregation in the South firmly defined social and cultural boundaries through Jim Crow laws, designed to enforce segregation, and mob violence. Even in New Orleans, with its history of close contact among ethnic groups, the policy of segregation prevailed. The black community responded with resentment and resistance. The famous case of *Plessy v.*

Ferguson involved a black Creole, Homer Plessy, who contested a Louisiana statute requiring "equal but separate" seating in railroad coaches. The U.S. Supreme Court upheld this statute in 1896.

What African Americans could not achieve in the courtroom they did achieve in the dance hall. Jazz music emerged as a form of rebellion, a direct challenge to the dominant white society. The blues music of rural black migrants, shaped by spirituals and work songs, merged with the music of dance halls, parades, rallies, and funerals played by New Orleans's working class, mostly African Americans, who became known for altering, or "ragging," their performances. By adding notes and embellishments and ornamentation, by using syncopation—irregular beats—and improvised ensemble playing, they produced a distinctive sound. Other ethnic groups, especially Afro-Creoles such as pianist Ferdinand "Jelly Roll Morton" LaMothe, trained in classical traditions and members of Italian and German brass brands joined in creating a vernacular music called ragtime.

Ragtime quickly spread from New Orleans around the country on riverboats and railroads and through the burgeoning sheet music publishing industry. While some ragtime performers offered more refined and structured variations, most black musicians in New Orleans continued to play with a raw, emotional, and rebellious spirit. The undisputed leader of this new music was Charles "Buddy" Bolden, an African American cornetist whose wild and exuberant style attracted a large following around 1900. His band played throughout the city, including black establishments like the Funky Butt Hall on Perdido Street, which featured ragtime that was loud, fast, and erotic. The highly sexualized dancing, raunchy humor, and heavy drinking associated with Bolden's performances established the identity of the new music. Although Bolden stopped performing before the word *jazz* appeared, around 1913, he is generally acknowledged as the first jazz musician.

The rise of Bolden and other pioneer jazzmen coincided with the establishment of Storyville, the notorious section of the city where prostitution was permitted and brothels catered to customers from plantations, city neighborhoods, riverboats, and merchant ships. From 1897 to 1917, Storyville became known not only for its brothels but also as an entertainment center with bars, dance halls, and gambling clubs. Jazz was not invented in Storyville, but it was there that musicians played it with great flare and intensity, and where audiences from around the world probably heard it for the first time.

Louis Armstrong grew up near Storyville and absorbed all the sounds that filled the city day and night. At fourteen, he got his first job, playing cornet in a bar. His big break came when Joe "King" Oliver, a prominent bandleader, became his mentor. By 1919, he was playing on summer riverboat excursions; three years later, Oliver invited him to join his band in Chicago. Other top jazz performers from New Orleans had also left the city—clarinetist Sidney Bechet to Europe; composer and pianist Jelly Roll Morton to Los Angeles and Chicago. Other bands headed to New York.

Armstrong dominated the jazz world in the 1920s. He developed a personal style, introducing solo performing and vocalizing. In 1927, he began playing the trumpet and demonstrated an incredible talent for his extended range—he once hit two hundred high Cs in a row! From 1925 to 1928, he and his groups, the Hot Five and Hot Seven, made eighty-nine legendary recordings, which established jazz as an art form. His 1928 duets with pianist Earl "Fatha" Hines were brilliant demonstrations of craftsmanship and innovation. His music influenced several generations from Duke Ellington to Wynton Marsalis. He also became a popular and beloved public figure throughout the world, the most recognized personality of the period that F. Scott Fitzgerald called "the Jazz Age."

In 1980, New Orleans dedicated Armstrong Park, a thirty-one-acre site bordering the French Quarter. The park features a statue of Armstrong by Elizabeth Catlett, a monument to jazz soloist Sidney Bechet, a memorial grove honoring twelve jazz pioneers, and the Mahalia Jackson Center for the Performing Arts. The site of Congo Square is located in the park as well as Municipal Auditorium, where Armstrong played annual concerts. It is a short walk to the former Storyville district in the Tremé neighborhood, where only a few historic buildings remain, including Lulu White's Saloon on Basin Street and Frank Early's "My Place" saloon on Bienville Street. The National Park Service offers tours of major sites related to jazz history.

The musical heritage of New Orleans is so powerful that it overshadows architectural treasures in the French Quarter, where the Historic New Orleans Collection has preserved several landmarks, and in the Garden District. Two French Quarter landmarks are the Cabildo, built in 1788 as Spain's government center when it controlled New Orleans and now a state museum, and Preservation Hall, where traditional New Orleans jazz is still performed. A few blocks away, in the warehouse district, excellent museums such as the National WWII Museum and the Ogden Museum of Southern Art are worth visiting.

The city's living historical traditions engage visitors. In spite of hurricanes and floods, scandals and crime, it is still "the Big Easy," with its leisurely pace, famous restaurants, and nonstop musical performances. Its residents have held on to and nurtured this heritage and its legacy of creativity, diversity, and resilience.

WEBSITES
New Orleans Jazz National Historical Park, www.nps.gov/jazz
Storyville, www.storyvilledistrictnola.com
Congo Square–Louis Armstrong Park, www.nola.gov/parks-and
    -parkways/parks-squares/congo-square-louis-armstrong-park
Preservation Hall, www.preservationhall.com
Ogden Museum of Southern Art, www.ogdenmuseum.org

NEARBY PLACES
The National WWII Museum, www.nationalww2museum.org
Louisiana State Museum, www.louisianastatemuseum.org
Oak Alley Plantation, www.oakalleyplantation.com
The Historic New Orleans Collection, www.hnoc.org
The Garden District, www.neworleanscvb.com/visit/neighborhoods

36

LEGENDARY HOLLYWOOD: WARNER BROS. STUDIO

BURBANK, CALIFORNIA

Midwest Street Lot, Warner Bros. Studio

On a sprawling 110-acre complex of offices, workshops, warehouses, soundstages, and outdoor sets, Warner Bros. Studio in Burbank houses, an entertainment empire. Movies made here and at other studios around Los Angeles created an international identity for the United States and made "Hollywood" synonymous with creativity, enterprise, and celebrity. There is a studio museum here as well, filled with a rich collection of costumes, props, and unique artifacts from movies such as *The Maltese Falcon*, *Dirty Harry*, and the Harry Potter series. Visitors can also tour outdoor sets that were used as the backgrounds for popular films such as *The Music Man* and *Blade Runner*. Motion pictures, invented by Thomas Edison and others in the 1890s, became popular in the early twentieth century, when many Americans had more time for inexpensive entertainment such as amusement parks, penny arcades, state fairs, vaudeville theater, and sporting events.

In Youngstown, Ohio, in 1903, Sam Warner, son of Jewish immigrants from Poland, purchased a movie projector and seven hundred feet of film for $150. With his brothers, Harry, Albert, and Jack, he showed films in small towns in Ohio and Pennsylvania. According to family legend, Sam was the projectionist and Harry and Albert rented theaters and sold tickets. Jack, the youngest brother, sang and danced before and after shows while their sister Rose played piano. One of the films they showed was Edwin S. Porter's *The Great Train Robbery*, among the first movies to tell a story.

In 1907, the Warners opened their first theater, an empty storeroom they named the Cascade, in New Castle, Pennsylvania, and joined a group of independent producers, distributors, and exhibitors in the rapidly expanding motion picture industry. Despite their early success, they realized that theater owners could never count on having enough quality films or on a reliable delivery schedule from producers. As a result, Harry Warner formed the Pittsburgh-based Duquesne Amusement Supply Company and began buying films and distributing them to theaters in western Pennsylvania. This early film exchange was so successful that the brothers later opened exchanges in Norfolk and Atlanta.

Distributing films through exchanges was profitable but producers continued to dominate the industry. In 1912, the Warners sold their film exchange and began making movies in a studio in Brooklyn, New York. Five years later, they moved to Hollywood, California, and had a major success with *My Four Years in Germany*, based on U.S. ambassador James Gerard's bestselling book. Movies starring John Barrymore and Rin Tin Tin, one of the first animals in a feature film, were also profitable.

Shortly after Warner Bros. Pictures incorporated in 1923, the brothers secured financial support from Goldman Sachs investment bank. Their most significant technical achievement was the world's first talking pictures. As early as 1925, Sam Warner worked with Western Electric's Bell Laboratories in New York to adapt their synchronized sound research. In 1927, the studio risked most of its resources to produce *The Jazz Singer*, starring Al Jolson. Audiences were thrilled when Jolson sang on-screen but were astounded when he said, "Come on, Ma, listen to this."

Profits from the "talkies" allowed Warner Bros. to purchase a network of film exchanges, a national chain of theaters, and the Burbank studio that still serves as its headquarters. During the Great Depression, the studio survived by producing movies on many subjects—classic stories such as *The Prince and the Pauper* and *The Adventures of Robin Hood*; realistic gangster movies such as *Little Caesar* with Edward G. Robinson and *Public Enemy* starring James Cagney; popular cartoons such as *Looney Tunes* and *Merrie Melodies*; and Busby Berkeley musicals such as *42nd Street* and *Gold Diggers of 1933*. Warner Bros. signed Bette Davis, Humphrey Bogart, and Ronald Reagan to long-term contracts. Even in the grim economy of the 1930s, producers, directors, and movie stars enjoyed great wealth, which they spent on lavish homes, clothes, jewelry, and parties. The media and the public adored Hollywood.

In response to the rise of fascism in Europe and concerns about social and economic justice in America in the 1930s, Warner Bros. was the first major studio to address contemporary issues in films like *Black Legion*, about a Ku Klux Klan splinter group; *Black Fury*, about the plight of coal miners; and *The Life of Emile Zola*, about the writer who exposed anti-Semitism in France.

The studio's most ambitious project during this period was *Confessions of a Nazi Spy*. Released in April 1939—five months before the start of World War II—the film tells the story of an international spy network directed by Adolf Hitler's government in Berlin. Using a documentary approach and newsreel footage showing German troops marching into Austria and Czechoslovakia, the film portrays the United States as unprepared to defend itself against German aggression. An FBI agent, played by Edward G. Robinson, dismantles the German spy ring. The movie ends with a dramatic courtroom scene and a warning about the threat of Nazi Germany.

Confessions provoked an intense reaction worldwide, banned in Germany, Japan, and more than twenty other countries. Many critics, however, congratulated Warner Bros. for breaking the conventional unwritten taboos against making films with political content. Most American movie studios at that time catered to middle-class values and promoted a relentlessly positive outlook. They feared government censorship, and their concerns persisted after World War II, when Cold War politics cast a shadow over the industry. Under the threat of McCarthyism and blacklists, Hollywood studios wavered between demonstrating patriotism and creating films with strong dramatic and sometimes controversial content.

In the 1950s, Warner Bros. went through a tumultuous period when the brothers fought over control of the iconic company they had built. Jack emerged as the studio's leader and continued as president and chairman until the late 1960s. Although there have been leadership and ownership changes in recent decades, Warner Bros. has retained strong connections to its roots by expanding into other forms of entertainment such as television and music and by adapting to new technologies like DVDs and Web-based media.

WEBSITES

Warner Bros. Entertainment, www.warnerbros.com

Walt Disney Studios, www.waltdisneystudios.com

Universal Studios, www.universalstudios.com

NEARBY PLACES

StarLine Tours' Movie Stars' Homes Tour, www.starlinetours.com
    /los-angeles-tour-1.asp

Hollywood Walk of Fame, www.walkoffame.com

37

FORD ROUGE

DEARBORN, MICHIGAN

Ford Motor Company Rouge Plant

When Henry Ford began building a massive new complex on the Rouge River in 1917, he was already the undisputed king of American industry. Ford did not invent the car; however, by mastering mass production technology and promoting mass consumption, he made the automobile the shaping technology of the twentieth century. Born on a small farm near Dearborn, Michigan, in 1863, he hated farmwork but loved to tinker with machines and small engines. In the 1890s, he worked as an engineer for the Edison Illuminating Company, and in his spare time he experimented with various types of self-propelled vehicles and internal combustion engines. Thomas Edison personally encouraged Ford and the two men later developed a close friendship.

Ford understood that success in manufacturing depended on appealing to America's growing middle class. In 1908, he introduced the Model T, a car that quickly gained popularity due to its durability, comfort, and low cost. In 1910, he moved the production of the Model T to a new factory at Highland Park, where, in 1913, the Ford Motor Company revolutionized production by applying assembly line technology to making automobiles. The result was an eightfold decrease in the time it took to produce a car, and, within a few years, a 50 percent decrease in its price.

These important changes paled in comparison to his announcement in 1914 that he would pay production workers five dollars for an eight-hour day. This was an unheard-of wage at that time. Not only did Ford receive credit for improving the lives of workers and their families, he also reaped the benefit of giving workers the ability to purchase his cars. Regardless of his motivations, Ford embodied the widely held belief that

everyone—owners, managers, workers—could share in the prosperity
and progress of the industrial revolution.

With his reputation at its peak in 1915, Ford began building a new
complex on a two-thousand-acre site along the Rouge River. His dream
was of a completely self-sufficient facility with all the resources needed to
produce complete automobiles. By 1927, when production began on a
new car, the Model A, Ford River Rouge was the most integrated factory
in the world. The entire complex included sixteen million square feet in
nearly a hundred buildings, many designed by Albert Kahn, the nation's
preeminent industrial architect. River Rouge had steel mills, ore docks,
coke ovens, glass factories, a paper mill, a tire-making plant, and plants
for engine casting, framing and assembly, radiators, and tool and die
making. An enormous power plant made so much electricity that Ford
sold the surplus to the city of Detroit. A fleet of ore freighters brought
raw materials—coal, timber, iron ore, and limestone—from properties
Ford owned in the upper Midwest.

Although no one lived at the Rouge, it had every attribute of a modern city—one hundred miles of railroad tracks, fifteen miles of paved
road, a fire department, a police force, a hospital, a maintenance crew
of 5,000 people, and, at its peak in the early 1930s, more than 100,000
workers.

Like most manufacturers, the Ford Motor Company responded to
the Great Depression by cutting wages, reducing hours, and laying off
thousands of workers. To represent workers against the big auto companies, a new union, the United Auto Workers (UAW), formed in 1935.
Sit-down strikes and other tactics forced General Motors and Chrysler
to recognize the union in 1937. Only Henry Ford resisted unionization.
He already had a record of conflict with his employees, using his Socio-
logical Department to collect personal information about workers and
his Service Department to enforce strict workplace discipline. On May
26, 1937, the company's security force severely beat a number of union
organizers, including Walter Reuther (later UAW president), outside the
River Rouge plant. This incident, known as the Battle of the Overpass,

attracted national attention and increased support for the union cause. It was not until 1941, however, that Ford finally recognized the union. By that time, River Rouge and other Ford plants were gearing up for the massive mobilization needed for World War II, when America became known as "the Arsenal of Democracy."

The conflicts with labor reinforced Ford's identity as an isolated and often eccentric figure, a very different image from the man hailed as a champion of the middle class. In the 1920s, for example, he supported a bitter anti-Semitic campaign in which he blamed Jews for his company's financial setbacks. Even as sales declined and rival General Motors assumed industry leadership, he refused to change the styling or color of the famous Model T. In 1927, the last Model T came off the assembly line, a relic of an earlier period of automotive history, after more than fifteen million had been produced.

Soon after it opened, River Rouge symbolized a technological revolution that inspired many artists. The Detroit Institute of Arts, with funds provided by Ford's son Edsel, commissioned Mexican artist Diego Rivera to produce a stunning series of murals called *Detroit Industry* that featured assembly line workers at River Rouge. Assisted by his wife, Frida Kahlo, Rivera completed the project in 1933. The same year, Henry Ford opened Greenfield Village, America's first open-air museum, near the River Rouge plant—a place where visitors could experience history through craft demonstrations and tours of historic buildings such as a one-room schoolhouse, a dairy barn, and the homes of famous Americans. In the heart of the village, he re-created the original laboratory of his hero, Thomas Edison. The village, Ford exclaimed, would "give people a true picture of the development of the country."

Today, the *Detroit Industry* murals are still displayed at the Detroit Institute of Arts. In Dearborn, Greenfield Village and the Henry Ford Museum are superb educational institutions visited by 1.6 million people each year. Beginning in 2004, visitors could also tour a section of the River Rouge plant to watch a high-tech assembly line in which 5,500 workers produce 1,200 F-150 pickup trucks each day, assisted by robots that do the heavy lifting. The plant aspires to be a model of sustainable and environmentally sound manufacturing, cleaning storm water, using plants to restore healthy soils, and providing more daylight and fresh air in the workplace. In many respects, the new River Rouge reflects the spirit of Henry Ford, a flawed revolutionary who profoundly changed American life in the twentieth century.

WEBSITES

Ford Rouge Factory Tour, www.thehenryford.org/rouge
The Henry Ford (museum), www.thehenryford.org/museum
Greenfield Village, www.thehenryford.org/village

NEARBY PLACES

Arab American National Museum, www.arabamericanmuseum.org
Historic Fort Wayne (Coalition), www.historicfortwaynecoalition.com
Motown Museum, www.motownmuseum.org
Detroit Institute of Arts, www.dia.org

38

WILL ROGERS HIGHWAY

CLAREMORE, OKLAHOMA

The Will Rogers Birthplace Ranch

On October 18, 1931, as the Great Depression gripped America, President Herbert Hoover asked Will Rogers to speak on a national radio broadcast for the President's Organization on Unemployment Relief (POUR) to solicit contributions for unemployed workers and their families. Rogers praised the president's efforts, then added, "The only problem that confronts this country today is at least seven million people are out of work. That's our only problem. . . . It's to see that every man that wants to is able to work . . . and also to arrange some way of getting more equal distribution of the wealth in the country."

Rogers could call for a redistribution of wealth and not be accused of being a socialist or un-American because he was possibly the most trusted man in the country, an honest advocate for the common man. He grew up in what was then Indian Territory near Claremore, Oklahoma, in a prominent Cherokee Nation family that had moved to the territory in the 1830s, just before the infamous Trail of Tears (the forced removal of 16,000 Cherokee from Georgia, a journey so arduous that four thousand people died along the way). Rogers's father owned a large ranch, where Will learned riding and roping skills from a former slave. He performed as "the Cherokee Kid" in circuses, rodeos, and vaudeville shows around the world, known for his distinctive outfits and his practical country wit and wisdom. In the hit musical *Oklahoma!*, Rodgers and Hammerstein based the show on a play called *Green Grow the Lilacs* by another Claremore native, Lynn Riggs, who used Will Rogers as the model for the character Will Parker.

In the 1920s and '30s, Rogers became a movie star, a radio commentator, and a syndicated columnist for the *New York Times* who reached forty million readers each week. He was compared to Mark Twain for his willingness to satirize powerful and famous people, yet his most quoted saying, "I never met a man I didn't like," summarized his basic optimism.

In 1935, in search of new material for his newspaper column, Rogers persuaded famed aviator Wiley Post to fly to Alaska. He was the sole passenger when Post's plane, a hybrid Lockheed Orion-Explorer, crashed near Point Barrow on August 15, killing both men. President Franklin D. Roosevelt led a stunned nation in mourning, noting that when Rogers "wanted people to laugh out loud, he used the methods of pure fun. And when he wanted to make a point for the good of mankind, he used the gentle irony that left no scars behind it." The Rogers family donated twenty acres in Claremore for a memorial and museum that today presents exhibitions and films. Visitors can also tour the Will Rogers Birthplace Ranch twenty miles north of town. Every August since 1989, there has been a "fly-in" on a small airstrip at the ranch honoring Post and Rogers. Oklahomans also honored him with a statue in Statuary Hall in the U.S. Capitol, and highway officials renamed Route 66, the road that ran through his hometown, the Will Rogers Highway.

Route 66 opened as a federal road in 1927 after Cyrus Avery from Tulsa, Oklahoma, and other businessmen lobbied for a road from Chicago to Los Angeles. The road, which included remnants of other routes, like the Pontiac and Santa Fe trails, eventually covered 2,448 miles through eight states. Avery and his associates publicized the road, called it "the Main Street of America," published guidebooks to it, and organized rodeos, festivals, and other events around it. One memorable promotion was the Trans-Continental Footrace, which covered the full length of Route 66 and continued east from Chicago to New York. In 1928, 275 runners paid $100 each to compete for a $25,000 prize. Andy Payne, an Oklahoman of Cherokee heritage, finished first in eighty-four days.

By the early 1930s, the popularity of Route 66 and other multistate roads reflected greater independence and mobility. Gas stations, diners, souvenir shops, and a new form of hospitality—the motel—catered to truckers, business travelers, and tourists. Attractions along Route 66 fostered an Old West theme, adopted Pueblo Indian and Spanish Colonial architecture styles, and sponsored festivals, craft demonstrations, and ceremonies based on regional history and culture even though Indians and Hispanics as well as African Americans were usually excluded from these attractions. In response to segregation, the Negro Motorist Green Book (published annually from 1936 to 1964) began listing places around the country that would accept minorities.

The identity of Route 66 changed again in the late 1930s. The Great Depression worsened in the Plains states when severe droughts transformed the region into the Dust Bowl, forcing thousands of farm families, collectively known as "Okies," to migrate west. Their experience found literary expression in John Steinbeck's novel *The Grapes of Wrath* (1939). Steinbeck described the plight of the Joad family on the perilous and uncertain journey to California. "Highway 66 is the main migrant road," he wrote. "66—the long concrete path across the country, waving gently up and down on the map. . . . [And] the people are in flight, and they come into 66 from the tributary side roads, from the wagon tracks and the rutted country roads. 66 is the mother road, the road of flight."

The peace and prosperity that followed World War II generated new enthusiasm for travel along Route 66. A popular song written by Bobby Troup in 1946 and recorded by Nat King Cole urged motorists to "get your kicks on Route 66," capturing the carefree, confident spirit of postwar America, as did a popular television series in the 1960s called *Route 66*. Beginning in 1956, however, the federal interstate highway program made Route 66 and other two-lane roads obsolete. With much of the road in disrepair and hundreds of attractions demolished or closed, Route 66 was decommissioned as a highway in 1985.

Preserving Route 66 is now the work of a national commission that coordinates eight state associations and documents the history of travel before the interstates, chain stores, and franchised restaurants altered the landscape. Oklahoma is the leader along this corridor with museums in Clinton and Elk City. There is a Route 66 Memorial in Tulsa that honors Cyrus Avery. Tulsa is also home to the Gilcrease Museum with its outstanding collection of western art and archives. The Woody Guthrie Center opened in 2013 with exhibits, archives, and recordings including "Will Rogers Highway" (1940). In many respects, Guthrie has overtaken his hero, Will Rogers, in our collective memory as the authentic voice advocating for those on the margins of society.

WEBSITES

Will Rogers Memorial Museums, www.willrogers.com

Rogers County Historical Society, www.rchs1.org

Route 66 Corridor Preservation Program, www.nps.gov/rt66

NEARBY PLACES

Trail of Tears National Historic Trail, www.nps.gov/trte

Gilcrease Museum, www.gilcrease.utulsa.edu

Woody Guthrie Center, www.woodyguthriecenter.org

Cyrus Avery Route 66 Memorial Bridge, vision2025.info/index.php
     /archives/2275

39

THE MOTHER CHURCH
OF COUNTRY MUSIC

NASHVILLE, TENNESSEE

Ryman Auditorium

Ryman Auditorium is called "the Mother Church of Country Music" by an industry that now dominates the economy and identity of Nashville, Tennessee. The religious reference is appropriate. Thomas Ryman built the Union Gospel Tabernacle Cathedral in 1892 for the Reverend Sam Jones's revival meetings. After Ryman died in 1904, Jones renamed the building in his honor. For forty years, the Ryman filled its three-thousand-seat galleries with religious programs, jazz concerts, operas, ballets, lectures, political debates, and boxing matches. Under the skillful management of Lula Naff, one of Nashville's few businesswomen at the time, the Ryman hosted leading performers such as Rudolph Valentino, Katharine Hepburn, Marian Anderson, and Bob Hope.

The turning point in the Ryman's history came in 1943 when Naff rented the hall on Saturday nights to the *Grand Ole Opry*, a live radio show on WSM 650, whose signal reached a loyal following throughout the South and, on clear nights, as far away as Chicago and Kansas City. The music—a blend of Appalachian mountain music, gospel, and African American blues—stirred its audience with simple, straightforward stories about lost love, family loyalty, and jobs in the mines, mills, and farms. With the R.J. Reynolds Tobacco Company as its main sponsor, the *Opry* enjoyed enormous regional success. Stars such as Jimmie Rodgers, Hank Williams, Patsy Cline, Bill Monroe, Minnie Pearl, and DeFord Bailey, the only African American musician in the *Opry*'s early days, performed at sold-out shows on Saturday nights, toured the region by bus during the week, and returned to the Ryman stage every Saturday to start the cycle again.

With a permanent and prestigious home at the Ryman Auditorium, the country music business flourished in Nashville after World War II. Young stars like Kitty Wells and Chet Atkins represented new directions. Wells was the first woman to sign a recording contract and achieve stardom on the *Grand Ole Opry.* Her biggest hit was "It Wasn't God Who Made Honky Tonk Angels" (1952), a song that expressed the needs and rights of women more than a decade before the modern feminist movement. Atkins first performed on the *Grand Ole Opry* in 1950 with the Carter Family. He recorded with Hank Williams and Elvis Presley and introduced the "Nashville sound," a fusion of country and popular styles like jazz, calypso, and Beatles tunes. As head of RCA Records, he built Nashville's reputation for creativity and quality production. Major artists like Ray Charles and Bob Dylan journeyed to Nashville to record with Johnny Cash and other musicians.

By the 1970s, the country music industry was a prime example of vertical integration. Instrument makers like Gibson Guitar and songwriters and music publishers like Acuff-Rose Publications located in the city. The Hatch Show Print shop, founded in 1879, preserved the art of letterpress printing, producing posters, lobby cards, and billboards to promote the latest shows. Major recording studios—RCA and Columbia—expanded along Music Row on Sixteenth and Seventeenth Avenues, employing the latest technology and sophisticated marketing. Led by Atkins, Owen Bradley, and the Country Music Association, country music became a global phenomenon.

The star performers moved their families to the city and spent their fortunes on new homes, big cars, and highly ornate fashion. The growth of country music fashion spurred the careers of immigrant designers such as Nudie Cohn from the Ukraine, Nathan Turk from Poland, and Manuel Cuevas from Mexico. Billed as "Nudie, the Rodeo Tailor," Cohn designed flashy rhinestone-studded clothing for Porter Waggoner and other stars. Turk introduced embroidery similar to designs from his homeland, with Buck Owens and the Maddox Brothers and Rose his best-known customers. Cuevas was head tailor and designer for Cohn and married his daughter. He started his own business, simply named

Manuel, with sewing machines from Turk, and moved to Nashville, making costumes for Roy Rogers, Dale Evans, and Johnny Cash.

With Nashville firmly established as its capital, country music spread to other cities including Austin, Texas, and Bakersfield, California. Shrewd promotion and marketing yielded sold-out concerts and soaring record sales. This success occurred in spite of the fact that country music, predominantly rooted in a white, rural, working-class audience, generated only a small following among African Americans and other ethnic minorities. Although many civil rights leaders came from Nashville, concerts at the Ryman Auditorium, like other venues in the South, remained racially segregated.

The Ryman became a victim of its own success. Its auditorium was too small and lacked air-conditioning and adequate dressing rooms. Furthermore, its neighborhood had declined and even loyal fans would not venture downtown. It closed in 1974 and the *Grand Ole Opry* moved to Opryland, a suburban theme park with a four-thousand-seat auditorium, a ballroom, hotel, and museum. The Ryman was at risk but advocates led by Historic Nashville Inc. rallied to save it.

With the exception of a rare concert or filming for a movie, the Ryman remained shuttered for twenty years. In 1994, after a five-year renovation, the auditorium reopened and regained its place as a center of popular music. Its rebirth coincided with the spectacular growth of Nashville as "Music City," a major destination for tourists from around the world. Initially, the city's social and cultural establishment resisted this trend. Once known as "the Athens of the South," the city promoted historic attractions such as Andrew Jackson's home, the Hermitage; its outstanding universities, Vanderbilt and Fisk; and its symphony orchestra. Country music was associated with working-class culture; nevertheless, tourists flocked to Opryland and the live music bars on Jefferson Street and Broadway, and filled the hotels, restaurants, and souvenir shops. They also made pilgrimages to the Ryman Auditorium and the Country Music Hall of Fame and Museum. Founded in 1961, the Hall of Fame collects and preserves the archives and artifacts of legendary performers. It offers tours of Historic RCA Studio B on Seventeenth Avenue, where Elvis Presley, Roy Orbison, the Everly Brothers, and Dolly Parton produced some of their greatest records. In 2014, the Hall of Fame opened a $100 million addition that doubled its size.

Despite the negative impact of digital music sharing on the recording industry, country music and other genres still define Nashville's identity. In the 1990s, the Visitor and Convention Bureau formally adopted the "Music City" brand and in 2009 won support for Music City Center, a $623 million project—the most expensive publicly financed complex in Tennessee's history—which includes 350,000 square feet of exhibition halls and a new hotel. With an undulating eco-roof that evokes the state's rolling hills and river valleys, and a central hall shaped like a guitar, the center represents the city's ambition and confidence that music tourism will continue to provide progress and prosperity.

WEBSITES
Ryman Auditorium, www.ryman.com
Grand Ole Opry, www.opry.com
Country Music Hall of Fame and Museum,
    www.countrymusichalloffame.org
Hatch Show Print, www.hatchshowprint.com

NEARBY PLACES
The Hermitage, www.thehermitage.com
Battle of Nashville, www.bonps.org
The Tennessee Historical Society, www.tennesseehistory.org

40

HOOVER DAM
BOULDER CITY, NEVADA

Hoover Dam

On September 30, 1935, President Franklin Roosevelt dedicated a mammoth dam on the Colorado River: "This morning I came, I saw and I was conquered, as everyone would be who sees for the first time this great feat. . . . Ten years ago the place where we are gathered was an unpeopled, forbidding desert. . . . The transformation wrought here is a twentieth-century marvel." Throughout his speech, FDR referred to the dam as "the Boulder Dam," the 727-foot behemoth designed to control floods, irrigate farmland, and generate electricity. Not once did he mention Herbert Hoover, his Republican rival in the 1932 presidential election, nor describe the key role Hoover played in building the dam. Not until 1947 did Congress officially approve the name Hoover Dam.

Hoover's claim on naming rights was strong. In 1922, he chaired a meeting at Bishop's Lodge in Santa Fe with representatives from seven states—California, Arizona, New Mexico, Colorado, Utah, Wyoming, and Nevada—to divide water rights in the Colorado River basin. Their compact, the first time more than two states ever signed a cooperative agreement, reflected mutual self-interests. The lower basin, especially Southern California, was growing rapidly, spurred by the oil industry, shipping, and agriculture. The less populous mountain and desert states feared losing access to water that passed through their boundaries to the policy of "prior appropriation" whereby the party that first uses a waterway has the right to it. Hoover, then secretary of commerce, negotiated a settlement that provided at least 50 percent of the annual river flow to the lower basin.

Ever since John Wesley Powell's explorations in 1869 and 1871 through the Grand Canyon, the Colorado had had a legendary reputation. Powell believed there was not enough water in the river basin to sustain unlimited growth. Despite his warning, westerners believed the river could drive economic expansion. In 1920, the U.S. Reclamation Service (renamed the U.S. Bureau of Reclamation in 1923) surveyed the river and recommended construction of a high dam in Boulder Canyon between Nevada and Arizona that would pay for itself through the sale of electricity. This report and the Colorado River Compact set the stage for the Hoover Dam.

In 1922, Congressman Phil Swing and Senator Hiram Johnson, both from California, drafted the Boulder Canyon Reclamation Act. Opposition came from various quarters: eastern states envious of California's prosperity; private utility companies that wanted to avoid competition with public agencies; and Harry Chandler, publisher of the *Los Angeles Times* and the wealthiest landowner in Southern California. Chandler opposed the dam because he feared it would have a negative impact on his already irrigated lands that covered more than 800,000 acres. However, popular support for the project kept building throughout the 1920s. Two catastrophes—the Mississippi River flood of 1927 and the St. Francis Dam collapse of 1928 near Los Angeles—provided further impetus for the dam. At the end of 1928, the Swing-Johnson bill finally passed. Not even the financial crisis of the Great Depression could derail this monumental public work. Herbert Hoover, elected president in 1928, continued to support the project and Franklin Roosevelt saw it as a symbol of the New Deal.

When the U.S. Bureau of Reclamation, whose staff designed Boulder Dam, issued a request for bids in 1931, no single construction company in America was big enough to handle the job. A consortium of companies, called Six Companies, Inc., won the contract by bidding $48,890,955, only $24,000 above the government estimate. One of the six was Kaiser-Bechtel of San Francisco, led by Henry Kaiser and Warren Bechtel, who would become major shipbuilders during WWII.

The Boulder Dam was located not in Boulder Canyon but in Black

Canyon, a site twenty miles downstream that proved to be more feasible. Even this site presented unprecedented technical challenges. Workers had to cut four diversion tunnels, each fifty-six feet in diameter, through Black Canyon. Skilled, courageous young workers called "high-scalers" swung through the canyon on cables to scrape away rock outcroppings, providing spectators with spectacular aerial shows. A project engineer invented a rig called the "drilling jumbo," consisting of scaffolding mounted on a flatbed truck that allowed thirty workers at a time to drill and plant explosives in the canyon walls. Eight jumbos operating in 1931 and 1932 moved the tunnel work forward at a record pace.

Recruiting and organizing a workforce was a major achievement. Frank Crowe, the project manager, assembled a crew that swelled to 5,241 men—with no Chinese allowed and very few African Americans—by 1934. Most lived in Boulder City, constructed especially for the project. Housing was cheap and wages—five dollars a day—were good in the depths of the Depression. Nevertheless, workers staged strikes in 1931 and 1935 in response to proposed wage reductions and dangerous working conditions. There were 112 deaths due to heat exhaustion, accidents, and electrocutions. The first was J. Gregory Tierney, a surveyor who slipped into the river on December 20, 1922. The last was his son, Patrick, who fell to his death on the same date in 1935.

Six Companies, Inc., finished Hoover Dam two years ahead of schedule and largely on budget. Its scale was stunning: 727 feet high and a base of 660 feet with more than 4.4 million cubic yards of concrete for the dam and powerhouse. Seventeen turbines generated more than 4.2 billion kilowatt hours annually. The dam created Lake Mead, a reservoir that stretched for 115 miles.

Hoover Dam was an aesthetic as well as an engineering triumph. The Bureau of Reclamation hired architect Gordon Kaufmann, who gave the dam its streamlined Art Deco appearance. Kaufmann recruited artist Allen Tupper True, who designed the terrazzo floor mural in the powerhouse, and sculptor Oskar Hansen, who created two 32-foot bronze statues flanking a 142-foot flagpole and a bas-relief workers memorial.

Hoover Dam and the more than two hundred dams that followed made urbanization possible in the Southwest. The lights of Las Vegas would not glow in the desert each night without energy from Hoover Dam. However, the consequences of uncontrolled growth have undermined the assumptions that caused these projects to be built. Experts now predict that in a few years, because of increased population, droughts, and climate change, there will not be enough water in the Colorado basin to sustain its cities and suburbs. They cite the prophecy of John Wesley Powell and the experience of the Ancestral Puebloans, who abandoned this region seven centuries ago.

Nevertheless, busloads of visitors take the guided tours of the dam and powerhouse and are, as Roosevelt predicted, "conquered" by the experience. Thirty miles west is Las Vegas, best known for its casinos but also home of the National Atomic Testing Museum, which tells the story of more than 350 nuclear tests in the nearby desert between 1946 and 1964. Perhaps it is fitting that this city sits near two of history's biggest technological and environmental gambles, nuclear warfare and damming the mighty Colorado.

WEBSITES

Bureau of Reclamation, Hoover Dam, www.usbr.gov/lc/hooverdam
Boulder City/Hoover Dam Museum, www.bcmha.org

NEARBY PLACES

National Atomic Testing Museum, www.nationalatomictestingmuseum
.org
Hispanic Museum of Nevada, www.hispanicmuseumnv.com
The Mob Museum, www.themobmuseum.org

41

PEARL HARBOR

HONOLULU, HAWAII

USS *Arizona* Memorial

Before asking Congress for a declaration of war on Japan for its attack on Pearl Harbor on December 7, 1941, President Franklin Roosevelt edited his prepared remarks. In the very first sentence he replaced "a date which will live in *world history*" with "a date which will live in *infamy.*"

Either phrase would have been appropriate. The surprise attack that left more than 3,500 Americans dead or wounded and crippled much of America's Pacific Fleet was one of the worst days in U.S. military history. It sparked the entry of the United States into a war that had already engulfed much of the world. For many historians, the Pearl Harbor attack and the German defeat by the Soviet Union at Stalingrad were turning points in the Allied victory in World War II.

Relations between the empire of Japan and the United States had worsened steadily for a decade as both countries sought to control resources and trade from China and Southeast Asia. In 1931, Japan invaded Manchuria, China's northernmost province. Six years later, Japanese troops attacked the rest of China and occupied Shanghai and Nanking. In response, the United States began an oil and raw-materials embargo to limit Japanese supplies for military operations. After war began in Europe in 1939, Japan entered into an alliance with Germany, Italy, and other Axis powers against England and her allies and took over French Indochina, further escalating the potential for conflict with the United States.

Despite continuing diplomatic efforts to avoid war, the Japanese concluded that the United States represented a major obstacle to its economic and military ambitions and adopted a strategy to immobilize

U.S. military outposts in Hawaii and other Pacific sites. In late November 1941, 33 warships, including 6 aircraft carriers with more than 350 planes, sailed from Japan under the command of Admiral Isoroku Yamamoto. Undetected by American intelligence, this force attacked Honolulu's Pearl Harbor on the morning of December 7. For two hours, waves of Japanese airplanes bombed American battleships as well as airfields and naval air stations. The USS *Arizona* sank after a 1,760-pound armor-piercing bomb struck it, causing an explosion that killed most of her crew.

The Americans counterattacked with Army Air Corps planes shooting down or disabling Japanese aircraft and sinking a few submarines. But this weak response in no way diminished the impact of the United States' catastrophic losses: 2,390 killed, 1,178 wounded, 21 battleships and other water craft destroyed or damaged, 323 planes destroyed or damaged.

In the next few months, the Japanese completed their conquest of the Pacific holdings of the European powers, the Dutch East Indies and the British colonies of Malaya, Hong Kong, and Singapore. They also invaded the Philippines, a U.S. territory, taking more than 75,000 American and Filipino prisoners and forcing General Douglas MacArthur into exile. By spring 1942, Japan had assembled one of the largest maritime empires in world history.

It had not, however, destroyed the U.S. capacity to rebuild its forces. The Pearl Harbor attack did not hit shipyards, fuel storage warehouses, or submarine bases. Most important, U.S. aircraft carriers were not in port on December 7 and were available for deployment. One carrier, the USS *Hornet*, launched a daring raid by B-25 bombers, led by Lieutenant Colonel Jimmy Doolittle, on Tokyo and other cities in April 1942. Two months later, the *Hornet* joined carriers, cruisers, submarines, and destroyers in the Battle of Midway—an atoll a thousand miles northwest of Hawaii—in which the Japanese lost four aircraft carriers. Only six months after Pearl Harbor, America had achieved a decisive victory that helped to determine the outcome of the Pacific war.

The attack on Pearl Harbor and the war against Japan sparked a national campaign of anti-Japanese propaganda. In February 1942, President Roosevelt signed Executive Order 9066 that led to the forced relocation of 120,000 mainland Japanese Americans to ten prison camps in seven states. But in Hawaii, where 40 percent of the population was Japanese, it was not physically or economically feasible to establish relocation camps. The entire island was under military command that placed severe restrictions on Japanese residents, including a prohibition against serving in the military.

Within a year, however, the Army created two units for Nisei, second-generation Japanese-Americans—the 100th Infantry Battalion and the 442nd Infantry Regimental Combat Team, known as the "Go For Broke" regiment—and called for volunteers. More than 10,000 Nisei men, eager to demonstrate their courage and patriotism, offered to serve, and the Army accepted around 3,000 for active duty. They fought in Italy, France, and Germany and ultimately earned the distinction as one of the most decorated infantry units in U.S. history. One member of the regiment, Lieutenant Daniel Inouye, lost his right arm in battle and later represented Hawaii for more than fifty years in Congress.

In 1959, Hawaii became the fiftieth state, and its volcanic landscape, beautiful beaches, and rich Pacific island culture draw visitors from around the world. Several museums near Pearl Harbor preserve the history of World War II, including the Pacific Aviation Museum Pearl Harbor on Ford Island, which still bears the scars of war; the battleship *Missouri*, where General MacArthur accepted the Japanese surrender in 1945; and the USS *Arizona* Memorial, dedicated in 1962, spanning the ruins of the battleship, now a watery grave for 1,177 men. The memorial designer, Alfred Preis, had fled his native Austria in 1939, moved to Honolulu, and briefly was one of 11,000 Germans and Italians detained after the attack. He designed a 183-foot white concrete box that slopes toward the center and rises at both ends, showing, as Preis intended, American resilience after the tragic losses of war. This place, visited by more than a million people each year, offers powerful testimony to the battle cry that rallied a nation: "Remember Pearl Harbor!"

WEBSITES

USS *Arizona* Memorial, www.nps.gov/usar

Pacific Historic Parks, www.pacifichistoricparks.org

Pacific Aviation Museum Pearl Harbor, www.pacificaviationmuseum
.org

Battleship *Missouri* Memorial, ussmissouri.org

NEARBY PLACES

Bernice Pauahi Bishop Museum, www.bishopmuseum.org

Iolani Palace, www.iolanipalace.org

42

MINIDOKA CAMP

JEROME, IDAHO

Minidoka National Historic Site

There was no poetry in camp
But the people made it so.
With hands, vision, hearts,
The people made it so.
—LAWSON FUSAO INADA, "Healing Gila, for The People"

The story of the Minidoka camp is one of injustice, perseverance, and redemption. This was a prison camp for thirteen thousand Japanese American citizens and legal aliens who were never even accused of crimes. After Japan's attack on Pearl Harbor, public fear of espionage and sabotage led President Franklin Roosevelt to issue Executive Order No. 9066 on February 19, 1942, which granted authority to military officials "to prescribe military areas in such places and of such extent . . . from which any and all persons may be excluded." In effect, the federal government used the executive order to define a broad corridor along the West Coast as "military areas" and to relocate Japanese Americans from that area.

General John L. DeWitt, western defense commander based at the Presidio in San Francisco, implemented this order through directives that forced the relocation of Japanese Americans living in West Coast communities. General DeWitt worked with the War Relocation Authority (WRA) and other agencies to find federal land for ten camps in seven states.

A few American leaders voiced concern about this policy. Milton Eisenhower, the brother of General Dwight Eisenhower and briefly director of the WRA, wrote that "when the war is over and we consider calmly this unprecedented migration of 120,000 people, we as Americans are going to regret the unavoidable injustices that may have been done." His dissent, however, could not overcome deep mistrust and racism toward Japanese Americans. For several generations, the Japanese had established themselves in many West Coast communities and achieved notable success in business, education, and the arts. But they still encountered discrimination and legal restrictions. After Pearl Harbor they faced an unprecedented wave of wartime hysteria, suspicion, and prejudice.

Residents at Minidoka came from Oregon, Washington, and Alaska. Allowed to travel with only a few personal belongings, they sold their homes and property at deep discounts and reported to makeshift assembly centers in fairgrounds and racetracks. One assembly center in Puyallup, Washington, named Camp Harmony, housed more than seven thousand people who were later transferred to Minidoka.

They arrived in August 1942 in the soaring heat of Idaho's high desert and encountered, in the words of one resident, "the land God had forgotten, a vast expanse of nothing but sagebrush and dust." The Army awarded Morris-Knudsen a $4.6 million contract to build residential barracks, warehouses, schools, a hospital, dining halls, and other facilities—600 buildings on 33,000 acres. The company employed more than 3,000 workers, including some Japanese American prisoners at severely reduced pay. Camp facilities initially lacked electricity, adequate plumbing, or proper medical care. The first winter was particularly difficult with subzero temperatures and dwindling supplies of coal for heating and cooking.

Conditions improved a little during the next year. By mid-1943, the camp reached its full size, containing nearly four hundred barracks, each designed to hold six families, although extended families—grandparents, aunts, and uncles—were often separated. The barracks were nothing more than tarpaper shacks 20 feet wide and 120 feet long without insulation.

A living quarter contained a woodstove, cots, a table, and little else. A single bulb provided light for the entire family. Communal showers and public toilets were in a separate laundry building. Armed guards patrolled, and at the beginning barbed wire surrounded the camp.

Somehow the prisoners at Minidoka persevered and created a vibrant community. They built ball fields and a swimming hole and cultivated flower gardens and parks with picnic areas. They held classes for camp children, sponsored musical events, and published a weekly newspaper. They irrigated a thousand acres of farmland, producing nearly enough food to feed the entire camp. Their religious faith, traditional family-centered values, and a prodigious work ethic sustained them through a painful ordeal. Most of the camp elders expressed a stoic philosophy—*Shikata ga nai* ("It cannot be helped")—during the darkest times.

Wartime labor shortages created the need for prisoners to work at neighboring farms and construction sites. One of these workers was George Nakashima, a skilled woodworker who gained recognition as a master craftsman in the decades following the war. Other notable camp residents were Kenjira Nomura, who painted scenes of Minidoka; Roger Shimomura, whose childhood memories of the camp influenced his painting; Monica Sone, author of *Nisei Daughter*, which describes her experience at Minidoka; and Mitsuye Yamada, a poet and activist who wrote *Camp Notes and Other Poems* as a reminder of the injustices and racism endured by Japanese Americans during the war.

Some young men and women at Minidoka served in the war when the U.S. Army allowed them to volunteer for military service in 1943. After passing loyalty tests in which they renounced allegiance to Japan and its emperor, most joined the 442nd Regimental Combat Team. Of the thousand men and women who served from Minidoka, two received the Medal of Honor. Seventy-three men died in combat.

Minidoka closed in October 1945 and some of the prisoners returned to the West Coast. Many had lost their homes and businesses. They tried to rebuild their lives but the experience of the camps was never forgotten. In the 1980s, a movement to recognize the injustice of the imprisonment and wartime service of Japanese Americans resulted in the Civil Liberties Act (1988), which granted reparations of $20,000 to all camp survivors. In 1991, President George H. W. Bush formally apologized, calling the government's action "a great injustice and it will never be repeated." In 1992, war veterans and camp survivors dedicated the Memorial to Japanese-American Patriotism in World War II in Washington, D.C.

Minidoka is a two-hour drive from the state capital of Boise. The most notable sites along this journey are near Hagerman, including a rich deposit of fossil horses, portions of the Oregon Trail, and the headquarters for the Minidoka National Historic Site. Minidoka itself is a remarkable place to visit in spite of its remote location and simplicity. The National Park Service has developed a 1.6-mile trail that offers views of the few surviving buildings—barracks, warehouses, a root cellar—informative kiosks with oral histories and historic photographs, and the walls of the guardhouse and visitors' waiting room. Most memorable is the Minidoka Honor Roll, a sign first dedicated in 1943 and reproduced by preservationists, that lists men and women who volunteered for military service, vivid testimony to their enduring loyalty even while family and friends were held captive in the high desert of Idaho.

WEBSITE
Minidoka National Historic Site, www.nps.gov/miin

NEARBY PLACES
Idaho State Historical Society, www.history.idaho.gov
Hagerman Fossil Beds National Monument, www.nps.gov/hafo

43

MANHATTAN PROJECT

RICHLAND, WASHINGTON

Hanford B Reactor

On August 2, 1939, Albert Einstein and Leo Szilard wrote a letter to President Roosevelt warning that scientists in Nazi Germany were probably working on "extremely powerful bombs" with unprecedented destructive force. Citing laboratory research in Europe and America, the letter noted "that it may be possible to set up a nuclear chain reaction in a large mass of uranium, by which vast amounts of power and large quantities of new radium-like elements would be generated." It urged Roosevelt "to speed up the experimental work" at American universities and establish formal contact between the government and the scientists working on nuclear research.

Einstein, perhaps the most famous scientist in the world, had emigrated from Europe as persecution of Jews and intellectuals by Adolf Hitler's government increased throughout the 1930s. Szilard, a Hungarian physicist, was first to conceive a nuclear chain reaction and the potential for an atomic bomb. An Italian physicist, Enrico Fermi, showed that splitting atoms, a process called fission, could trigger a nuclear explosion. Creating an atomic bomb involved the fission or splitting of the atom's nucleus, which produces a great deal of energy and releases atomic particles that split other atoms in a chain reaction. A large enough chain reaction, delivered in a bomb, would generate enormous amounts of heat and radiation capable of destroying whole cities. Most chemical elements—hydrogen, oxygen, iron, lead—were stable, but in 1938 German scientists discovered that uranium, especially uranium-235, split more easily than other elements. In 1940, Glenn Seaborg and scientists at the University of California, Berkeley, produced another fissionable element, plutonium, that could be used in a nuclear weapon. At laboratories in

New York, Chicago, and Washington scientists produced chain reactions using uranium and plutonium.

Even before the United States entered World War II, President Roosevelt promised that the country would be an "Arsenal of Democracy." During the war, America's factories produced 1,556 naval ships, 5,777 merchant ships, 88,410 jeeps, 2,383,311 trucks, 6.5 million rifles, 40 billion bullets, and 299,293 airplanes. Winning the war depended on the mobilization of millions of workers, and a wartime spirit engulfed America's home front. Production of the atomic bomb involved a top-secret operation that would involve thousands of people at multiple sites. In early 1942, the Army Corps of Engineers established a command center at 270 Broadway in New York to manage this program. The Manhattan Engineer District, better known as the Manhattan Project, operated under the leadership of General Leslic R. Groves, a remarkable and dynamic officer responsible for assembling interdisciplinary teams—physicists, chemists, mathematicians, engineers, and metallurgists—and selecting sites to produce the bomb. To serve as scientific director for the project, Groves selected J. Robert Oppenheimer, a brilliant and charismatic theoretical physicist at the University of California, Berkeley. Oppenheimer persuaded Groves to locate the principal laboratory and production facility in Los Alamos, New Mexico. Another Manhattan Project facility, located in Oak Ridge, Tennessee, produced small quantities of plutonium in a pilot reactor and eventually employed 75,000 workers to produce enriched uranium.

The third Manhattan Project site was 670 square miles of sagebrush and desert near Hanford in southeastern Washington, which met the criteria for security and safety—a remote area at least twenty miles from a major town and ten miles from a highway. Furthermore, the nearby Columbia River offered an abundant supply of fresh water and the recently built Grand Coulee Dam provided the electricity needed to manufacture plutonium. In 1943, the Army evicted three thousand people living in Hanford and neighboring communities. Members of the Wanapum and other Indian tribes who had fished, hunted, and camped along the Columbia River for centuries now had only limited access to the site.

To build Hanford Engineering Works, an undertaking that ultimately cost $350 million, General Groves and his on-site director, Colonel Franklin Matthias, contracted the DuPont Company of Wilmington, Delaware. In just eighteen months, DuPont hired nearly fifty thousand workers to build and operate a complex for fuel fabrication, reactor operations, and chemical separation.

The reactor core was a cube, thirty-six feet wide and high, made of graphite blocks and produced 250 million watts of heat as it radiated the fuel. Water from the Columbia River cooled the reactor and a pool outside the plant cooled the spent fuel elements. By early 1945, Hanford Engineering had produced enough plutonium—fourteen pounds—for use in an atomic bomb.

In spring 1945, Germany and its European allies surrendered. President Roosevelt died and his successor, Harry Truman, wanted to defeat Japan as quickly as possible. Although atomic bombs could quickly end the war, there was debate about whether to use them. Some American diplomats and scientists, including Leo Szilard, urged President Truman first to demonstrate this powerful new weapon to the Japanese. Other advisors argued that a demonstration might fail and the Pacific war could drag on indefinitely.

Truman approved a secret test and on July 16, 1945, the "gadget" using plutonium was successfully tested at the Trinity Site near Alamogordo, New Mexico. On August 6, the B-29 Superfortress *Enola Gay* dropped a bomb using enriched uranium over Hiroshima, Japan, and three days later a B-29 named *Bockscar* detonated a second bomb over Nagasaki using plutonium produced at Hanford. These attacks instantly killed more than 100,000 people and many more people died in the days, months, and years that followed. Japan formally surrendered on September 2. Truman never publicly regretted his decision but the debate over the use of nuclear weapons has persisted to the present day.

The Hanford site, managed after the war by General Electric and other contractors, continued to manufacture plutonium, more than thirteen thousand tons before operations ended in 1988. As a massive cleanup operation, the largest Superfund project in history, winds down, the process of preserving Hanford's story is under way. A new museum and cultural center in neighboring Richland opened in 2014 with exhibitions about the Manhattan Project. Guided tours by the Department of Energy include the hulking B Reactor; the enormous chemical plant, nicknamed "the Queen Mary"; and prewar buildings—a bank, a school, a pump house, a farmhouse—that survived army bulldozers. Mostly, however, it is the empty spaces where workers' barracks and production plants once stood that stir the imagination. Along the Columbia River, the scene is peaceful, much as when glaciers melted and the Wanapum hunted and fished. It is as if the dramatic events that launched the nuclear age never happened.

WEBSITES
Atomic Heritage Foundation, www.atomicheritage.org
Hanford Reach National Monument, www.fws.gov/refuge/hanford-reach
Manhattan Project B Reactor Tours, manhattanprojectbreactor.hanford
   .gov

NEARBY PLACES
Yakama Nation Museum & Cultural Center, www.yakamamuseum
   .com

44

SWEET AUBURN

ATLANTA, GEORGIA

Historic Ebenezer Baptist Church

Dr. Martin Luther King Jr. was arguably the most influential American of the twentieth century, the architect and symbol of the movement that challenged long-held assumptions about race, religion, and civil rights. Although he cited many people, places, and events that shaped his life, he acknowledged that the years he spent as a youth and young man at Ebenezer Baptist Church in Atlanta had the strongest impact.

He was born Michael King Jr. in 1929, but his father changed both their names in 1934 to honor German Protestant reformer Martin Luther. His maternal grandfather, A. D. Williams, was senior pastor at Ebenezer for thirty-seven years (1894–1931) and oversaw construction of a new sanctuary in 1914. His father married the Reverend Williams's daughter and became senior pastor in 1931. Although "Daddy" King was more conservative than his son on theological matters, he embodied the activist role that ministers played in the African American community, where Christian faith and values gave strength to people who had shared the hardships of slavery and then the constraints of segregation. From the pulpit, black preachers were influential as they addressed contemporary as well as religious issues. They also served as the contact points for the white community, which courted their support on social, cultural, and political matters. The example of Daddy King shaped Martin's understanding of a minister's important position in the community.

King enrolled at Morehouse College in Atlanta, a prestigious African American school for men whose graduates included leaders in education, science, government, and culture. There, he developed close ties with Dr. Benjamin E. Mays, the school's president and an outspoken critic of racial segregation. Under Mays's guidance, King made the decision to become a minister. He continued his education at Northern schools, Crozer Theological Seminary in Chester, Pennsylvania, and Boston University, where he received a doctorate and absorbed the liberal theology of Reinhold Niebuhr and Paul Tillich.

In 1953, he married Coretta Scott, a native of Alabama and a graduate of Antioch College in Ohio. She was a strong influence on her husband and his evolving philosophy of social justice. They settled in Montgomery, Alabama, where Dr. King became pastor of the Dexter Avenue Baptist Church in 1954, the same year the U.S. Supreme Court issued its *Brown v. Board of Education* decision, which replaced the philosophy of "separate but equal" with the constitutional doctrine of "equal protection." As a young, well-educated minister in the capital city of a segregated state, King was in an excellent position to shape race relations.

He did not have to wait long for the opportunity. On December 1, 1955, Montgomery police arrested an African American woman, Rosa Parks, for refusing to give up her seat on a bus to a white man, a violation of a local ordinance. News of her arrest spread quickly and African Americans responded with a bus boycott. A new organization, the Montgomery Improvement Association, invited Dr. King to serve as its president. King recognized that he was about to accept a role that would profoundly change his ministry and his life. He later wrote about a vision he had as he prayed one night in his kitchen contemplating the risks and dangers for himself and his family. Over the next year, the young minister grew more confident and effective in his leadership. He also became an advocate of peaceful nonviolence as practiced by Mohandas Gandhi, whose campaign of civil disobedience had ended colonial rule in India in 1948.

The Montgomery bus boycott ended on December 21, 1956—after lasting 385 days—when the U.S. Supreme Court ruled against the city ordinance requiring segregation on city buses. The boycott received national attention and launched Dr. King as a spokesman for the burgeoning civil rights movement. To encourage more organizing, he and other ministers met at Ebenezer Baptist Church in January 1957 to establish the Southern Christian Leadership Conference. For the next decade, this group and other such organizations transformed the nation's consciousness.

The civil rights movement ultimately succeeded but not without a series of hard-fought battles. Dr. King assumed a central role in many of these dramatic events. In 1957, he publicly encouraged President

GARY TARLETON, NATIONAL PARK SERVICE, HFC

Martin Luther King Jr. Birth Home

Eisenhower to intervene in the crisis over school integration in Little Rock, Arkansas. In 1963, he led thousands of students in a desegregation protest campaign in Birmingham, Alabama, where he landed in jail, one of thirty arrests in his life. From his jail cell, he defended his activism in a letter to fellow clergymen. "Injustice anywhere is a threat to justice everywhere," he wrote, and closed with the hope "that the dark clouds of racial prejudice will soon pass away . . . and in some not too distant tomorrow the radiant stars of love and brotherhood will shine over our great nation." Later that year, he led the March on Washington for Jobs and Freedom and, on the steps of the Lincoln Memorial, delivered a speech that has endured as one of the greatest in American history.

King won the Nobel Peace Prize in 1964, the same year Congress passed the Civil Rights Act, ending segregation in public facilities. The following year, he attended another historic ceremony as President Johnson signed the Voting Rights Act. That legislative victory came only after King and his followers had suffered a violent attack in Selma, Alabama, as they tried to march to Montgomery to promote voter registration. They resumed the march and entered Montgomery on March 25 a full decade after Dr. King began his ministry in that city.

In the mid-sixties, King shifted his attention to the movement opposing the Vietnam War. He also became an advocate for the rights of America's underclass, people living in poverty and the working poor. This issue brought him to Memphis, Tennessee, in April 1968, where an assassin's bullet ended his life. He was thirty-nine years old.

King's legacy is recognized in many ways. His birthday is a national holiday and a memorial on Washington's National Mall honors his achievements. In Atlanta, a national historic site includes a visitor center, guided tours of King's Birth Home, the tomb of Dr. and Mrs. King, and a Peace Rose Garden. The King Center for Nonviolent Social Change is nearby. These sites are in the Sweet Auburn neighborhood, the historic commercial, social, and cultural center of African American life in Atlanta. Historic Ebenezer Baptist Church, at 407 Auburn, is open for self-guided tours where a visitor can contemplate the extraordinary journey of a studious young man of modest origins, devoted to his faith, who changed America.

WEBSITES

Martin Luther King Jr National Historic Site, www.nps.gov/malu
Historic Ebenezer Baptist Church, www.historicebenezer.org

NEARBY PLACES

The Martin Luther King, Jr. Center for Nonviolent Social Change,
    www.thekingcenter.org
Center for Civil and Human Rights, www.civilandhumanrights.org
Atlanta History Center, www.atlantahistorycenter.com
Jimmy Carter Presidential Library and Museum,
    www.jimmycarterlibrary.gov

45

CENTRAL HIGH SCHOOL

LITTLE ROCK, ARKANSAS

Little Rock Central High School

A famous photograph of a white teenaged girl screaming at a black girl on their first day of school is an enduring image in civil rights history. The white girl, Hazel Bryan, had joined her classmates to protest the arrival of Elizabeth Eckford and eight other black students—the Little Rock Nine—as they tried to desegregate Central High School in Little Rock, Arkansas. The date was September 4, 1957, more than three years after the historic Supreme Court decision on *Brown v. Board of Education*, which found separate schools based on race unequal and unconstitutional. Despite a second court ruling urging integration "with all deliberate speed," school districts throughout the South resisted the court's decision. With few exceptions, desegregation ground to a halt.

Little Rock was an unlikely place for racial conflict. Although racism persisted, many public facilities—buses, parks, the city zoo—were no longer segregated. African Americans lived in a relatively peaceful atmosphere without the hostility and violence that occurred in many Southern communities. The one major exception to progress in race relations was public education. Little Rock invested heavily in segregated schools. For decades, its whites-only Central High School was a source of community pride. When it opened in 1927 at a cost of $1.5 million, it was the most expensive public school in the country. The American Institute of Architects called it "America's Most Beautiful High School," an imposing structure blending Art Deco and Collegiate Gothic styles.

In contrast, African American students attended schools that underscored their second-class status. They read from used textbooks in overcrowded classrooms. Yet there was great support for education in the African American community. Teachers were held in high regard and enjoyed parity in salary with their white counterparts. One of the African American schools, Dunbar High School, had the added distinction of being a Rosenwald school, financed in part through a remarkable program that constructed black schools throughout the South. Julius Rosenwald, president of Sears, Roebuck and Co., launched this initiative, the Rosenwald Fund, with the encouragement of Booker T. Washington, a leading national figure in the black community and founder of Tuskegee Institute in Alabama. Between 1911 and 1932, the fund's matching grants totaled $4.3 million, supporting construction of 4,977 schoolhouses, 217 homes for teachers, and 163 shop buildings.

Dunbar was one of the few urban schools funded through the Rosenwald Fund. Built in 1929 at a cost of $400,000 with almost $100,000 from grants from the Rosenwald Fund and the Rockefeller Fund, the school opened as a vocational school but later shifted its emphasis toward liberal studies consistent with the legacy of its namesake, the black poet Paul Lawrence Dunbar. Six of the Little Rock Nine attended Dunbar (after it became a junior high school) and all nine were enrolled at Horace Mann High when they volunteered to desegregate Central.

The Little Rock School Board was among the first in the South to adopt a gradual integration plan that would begin in 1957. As the date neared for the first day of school, opposition from the white community mounted. The Mothers' League of Central High School met on August 27 and briefly won an injunction against the plan. On September 2, Arkansas governor Orval Faubus announced that he had ordered National Guard troops to prevent the Little Rock Nine from entering Central. When the students arrived on September 4, an angry mob confronted them and the National Guard turned the students away. Fearing for their safety, the nine black teenagers waited nearly three weeks before renewing their attempt to attend Central High School. On September 23, they entered the school while a howling crowd of more than a thousand people filled the streets. Little Rock police, determined to prevent a riot, sent the children home.

Now the situation in Little Rock had become a national crisis, a confrontation between mob violence and the rule of law, a test of federal authority. Furthermore, these events took place at the height of the Cold War, the ideological and military competition between the United States and the Soviet Union. The picture of Hazel Bryan taunting Elizabeth Eckford appeared in publications and on television screens around the world, badly tarnishing America's reputation as a land of freedom and opportunity.

On September 24, President Eisenhower addressed the nation and called the situation in Little Rock "disgraceful," and added that "a foundation of our American way of life is our national respect for law." At the request of Little Rock's mayor, the president sent a thousand federal troops from the 101st Airborne Division to protect the students and took control of the state National Guard. This unprecedented display of federal power, one of the highlights of Eisenhower's presidency, restored order.

On September 25, the students peacefully entered Little Rock Central High School. With courage and dedication, they endured a difficult year, harassed by white students, isolated in the cafeteria, and unable to participate in school activities. Eight of the nine students finished the year (Minnijean Brown was expelled in 1958) and the lone senior, Ernest Green, graduated in May 1958 with Martin Luther King Jr. in the audience. By that time, however, Little Rock was a deeply divided city. The school board closed the schools for the 1958–59 year. This action galvanized new organizations such as the Women's Emergency Committee to Open Our Schools to support a referendum that removed segregationist school board members and paved the way for full school integration in 1959.

The deep wounds of the Little Rock crisis slowly healed. Over time, the city recognized the historical significance of the battles of the 1950s. With support from city and state officials, Central High School became a National Historic Site in 1998. Today, it remains an operating high school; the National Park Service schedules tours and manages a visitor and education center across the street. A driving tour includes the home of Daisy Bates, a community activist who recruited and mentored the Little Rock Nine, and Dunbar Junior High, now a magnet middle school.

A memorial depicting the Little Rock Nine, dedicated in 2005, now stands outside the State Capitol, where Governor Faubus once defended segregation. The route to the memorial from Central High follows Daisy Bates Drive and Martin Luther King Jr. Drive, further evidence of Little Rock's conscious effort to honor the history of civil rights.

The ceremonies and reunions honoring the Little Rock Nine have featured former president Bill Clinton, who acknowledges that as a young boy growing up in Arkansas he drew inspiration from their courageous example. The Clinton Presidential Library (2004), located along Little Rock's waterfront, frequently sponsors exhibitions and programs about civil rights history.

In 1997, following the fortieth reunion, Hazel Bryan and Elizabeth Eckford met again, not as adversaries but as middle-aged women seeking reconciliation. After that meeting, they spoke publicly about the need for racial tolerance. Their story and the infamous photograph that shaped their lives represent the crucible of race that defines so much of American history.

WEBSITES

Little Rock Central High School National Historic Site, www.nps.gov
   /chsc
Little Rock Nine Foundation, www.littlerock9.com
The William J. Clinton Presidential Library & Museum,
   www.clintonlibrary.gov

NEARBY PLACES

Mosaic Templars Cultural Center, www.mosaictemplarscenter.com
Arkansas History Commission, www.ark-ives.com

46

SALK INSTITUTE

LA JOLLA, CALIFORNIA

The Salk Institute

When Jonas Salk founded the institute that bears his name in La Jolla, California, he challenged Louis Kahn to "create a facility worthy of a visit by Pablo Picasso." By any standard, Kahn met and even exceeded expectations. The Salk Institute for Biological Studies, a genuine collaboration between client and architect, represents both the healing promise of medical research and the healing power of architecture.

Salk and Kahn shared similar histories and common experiences. Both were sons of poor Jewish immigrants and were considered outsiders in their respective fields. They were idealists who promoted humane values and challenged prevailing trends and assumptions before gaining international acclaim for their innovations and achievements.

Salk achieved international fame for developing a vaccine to prevent polio, a highly contagious, often crippling disease. He and other scientists received support from the National Foundation for Infantile Paralysis, later called the March of Dimes. President Franklin Roosevelt, the country's best-known polio survivor, started the foundation in 1938. His law partner, Basil O'Connor, served as foundation president and organized a fund-raising campaign by concentrating on small donations—pennies, nickels, and dimes—from children and people at all income levels. This grassroots effort represented a new approach to philanthropy. By the mid-1940s, the March of Dimes was a major force in funding medical research. In 1946, a year after Roosevelt died, his profile replaced the image of Mercury on America's ten-cent coin.

In 1947, after more than a decade studying the causes of influenza, Salk became director of the Virus Research Laboratory at the University of Pittsburgh School of Medicine. He believed that the same principle of inoculation used to prevent smallpox and rabies could apply to infectious diseases like polio. However, unlike the vaccines that used live viruses to build immunity, Salk maintained that a killed virus with a small amount of poliovirus would prevent a person from being infected. Building on research by scientists in labs worldwide, Salk and his team worked on the killed-virus theory. They redoubled their efforts when a polio epidemic hit in the early 1950s with almost 100,000 cases reported in 1952 and 1953.

Salk benefited from the work of Harvard researchers John Enders, Thomas Weller, and Frederick Robbins, who discovered how to produce enough poliovirus to manufacture a vaccine. He also overcame the skepticism of Albert Sabin and other scientists who doubted a killed-virus vaccine would provide lifetime protection against polio. Salk went ahead with trials first by injecting monkeys with the vaccine as well as patients who already had polio. He also inoculated himself, his staff, and his family. None of these volunteers developed polio.

In 1954, he launched a nationwide program involving one million children, "Polio Pioneers," with half receiving the actual vaccine and half receiving a placebo. On April 12, 1955—the tenth anniversary of Franklin Roosevelt's death—the vaccine was declared "safe, effective, and potent." Church bells rang across the country in celebration!

Salk's vaccine largely eliminated polio in the United States, and he ranked along with Churchill and Gandhi as one of the world's most admired people. Although he received many awards and prizes, neither he nor his colleagues profited from their discoveries. As he once asked in an interview, "How do you patent the sun?"

In the late 1950s, Salk turned his attention to creating an independent, interdisciplinary laboratory, an institute that would be a model of collaborative research. To build it, he needed a site, money, and a plan. The proposed site came from Charles Dail, the mayor of San Diego and a polio survivor, who offered a twenty-seven-acre parcel overlooking the Pacific Ocean near a new University of California campus. Seed money came from the March of Dimes.

The plan came from Louis Kahn, a respected professor at the University of Pennsylvania known principally for residential projects around Philadelphia. After World War II, Kahn took commissions for educational and public buildings, and developed a new approach to modern architecture. Inspired by the classical traditions of Rome, Greece, and Egypt, he combined historical and contemporary styles. In addition, he promoted the idea that buildings should serve a spiritual and social purpose.

The Salk Institute incorporated in 1960, began research activities in 1963, and moved into its new home in 1967. In more than fifty years, the institute has trained 2,700 scientists, 5 of whom are Nobel Laureates, who work on collaborative projects in genetics, biology, and neuroscience. Its presence in La Jolla contributes to the region's reputation as a center for scientific research and its architecture has inspired a number of important buildings, most notably the University of California, San Diego's Geisel Library by William Pereira (1970).

Nothing, however, surpasses Louis Kahn's design. Two rectangular concrete buildings house six sun-lit laboratories, designed to encourage maximum flexibility and interdisciplinary collaboration. Office towers with ocean views are attached to the main buildings. To promote greater social interaction, Kahn separated laboratories from offices. "I realized," he wrote, "that there should be a clean air and stainless steel area, and a rug and oak table area." To further emphasize the distinction between work space and social space, he placed offices overlooking gardens that lined the courtyard and used wood extensively in offices and exterior surfaces. A central courtyard, set in travertine marble divided by a narrow waterway, occupies the heart of the complex, offering outdoor meeting space in a stunning California landscape. Without trees or gardens obstructing the view, the courtyard is open to the ocean and the sky.

Kahn designed several other landmark buildings, including the Phillips Exeter Academy Class of 1945 Library in Exeter, New Hampshire; the Kimbell Art Museum in Fort Worth, Texas; and the National Parliament House of Bangladesh. Many projects were never built, largely due to shortfalls in funding. Fortunately, the University of Pennsylvania preserves an extensive archive of drawings, correspondence, and models. Among Kahn's unbuilt designs are a meetinghouse and a residence hall at the Salk Institute. Nevertheless, the institute remains one of America's greatest buildings. Although it is a working laboratory, visitors can schedule guided tours and draw inspiration from the living legacy of two men who saw the infinite possibilities of science and art.

WEBSITES
Salk Institute for Biological Studies, www.salk.edu

NEARBY PLACES
Geisel Library, University of California, San Diego, www.libraries.ucsd
    .edu
Mt. Soledad Veterans Memorial, www.soledadmemorial.com
Museum of Contemporary Art San Diego, www.mcasd.org
La Jolla Historical Society, www.lajollahistory.org

47

SATURN V ROCKET

HUNTSVILLE, ALABAMA

Saturn V

On May 2, 1945, in the Bavarian town of Schattwald, a young man on a bicycle rode up to American troops and announced, "We are a group of rocket specialists up in the mountains. My brother invented the V-2. We want to surrender." The young man was Magnus von Braun and his brother was Wernher von Braun, director of Germany's V-2 missile program. Within a few years, von Braun would be directing the U.S. space program and the team that designed the Saturn V rocket, the most powerful ever built. From 1964 to 1973, the United States used Saturn V rockets for thirteen missions, including six lunar landings. On July 20, 1969, a Saturn V–powered rocket launched Apollo 11, which landed on the moon, and two astronauts, Neil Armstrong and Buzz Aldrin, became the first people to walk on its surface.

Finding von Braun and the other German engineers and scientists was an important objective for the Americans. They needed to locate German weapons, to learn how they were made, and to find this information before the Soviet Union did. They called their program Operation Paperclip, reflecting the extensive files maintained on German scientists. Once they had custody of von Braun, American officials had a difficult decision to make. They could consider him and his colleagues prisoners of war and charge them with war crimes in light of their work on behalf of the Nazi regime on rocket missiles used against Britain and other countries during the war. On the other hand, America needed their expertise to develop the next generation of weaponry.

For five years, the von Braun brothers and 116 German engineers worked as alien employees at Fort Bliss near El Paso, Texas, where they tested rockets at the White Sands Proving Ground in New Mexico. In

1950, the Army relocated the rocket research program to Redstone Arsenal in Huntsville, Alabama, a good site for classified research. It was federally owned land, a former Army chemical depot with many empty munitions assembly buildings and lots of acreage for future growth. And most decisively, Huntsville was the home of Alabama's junior senator, John Sparkman, who sought more military spending in his state.

At Redstone, Wernher von Braun guided the American rocket program. A brilliant physicist and engineer, he was also a talented leader and administrator. Although he had spent his career designing missiles as weapons, his lifelong dream was to adapt this technology for space exploration. The opportunity came on October 4, 1957, when the Soviet Union launched Sputnik, the first satellite to orbit the earth.

The United States quickly responded to the success of Sputnik. In December 1957, von Braun's team started work on the Jupiter and Saturn rocket systems. In 1958, Congress established the National Aeronautic and Space Administration (NASA), and within a year, all space-related programs were transferred from the Army to NASA. In 1960, President Eisenhower came to Huntsville to dedicate the Marshall Space Flight Center, named for General George C. Marshall, the former secretary of state, whose Marshall Plan rebuilt Europe after World War II. In May 1961, President Kennedy pledged full support to "landing a man on the moon and returning him safely to earth" by 1970.

The national commitment to the space program reflected Cold War priorities, intelligence and defense, as well as the need for scientific research. Most important, Kennedy believed it was feasible to land a man on the moon before the Soviet Union and thus reap the benefits of international prestige. Congress followed his lead and approved enormous funding for NASA. After testing smaller rockets, NASA announced plans to build Saturn V, a rocket powerful enough to launch Apollo 11 for a moon landing.

Saturn V was an engineering marvel. At 363 feet—taller than the Statue of Liberty—and 6.2 million pounds, it towered over other rockets. A three-stage rocket with multiple engines fueled by liquid hydrogen, it utilized a Lunar Orbit Rendezvous (LOR), in which a small modular spacecraft separated from the main spacecraft, landed on the moon, and linked up with the main spacecraft before returning to Earth. More than 20,000 contracting companies—led by Boeing, North American Aviation, Douglas Aircraft, and IBM—fabricated 3 million parts that made up 700,000 components in a single rocket. The cost of the program over nine years totaled $6.5 billion, the equivalent of $46 billion in 2013. The only comparable government program in ambition, complexity, and expense was the Manhattan Project, which produced the atomic bomb.

The cost of the program led to its demise. After the lunar landings that followed Apollo 11, Americans lost enthusiasm for the space race and questioned the scientific value of manned flights. Subsequent ventures—Skylab, Spacelab, the Space Shuttle, and the International Space Station—have been productive and less costly.

In Huntsville, NASA's Marshall Space Flight Center continues to develop and test space vehicles and supports research on rocket engines and new ways to live and work in space such as the Space Launch System. The U.S. Space & Rocket Center, located a few miles away, offers bus tours around the center and Redstone Arsenal. The Rocket Center, established in 1970 by the Alabama legislature, provides educational programs about the history of space exploration and displays a rich collection of space technology. The center is the home of Space Camp, an experiential learning program for teachers and families. The highlight of a visit to the center is an original National Historic Landmark Saturn V rocket, used in the 1960s for vibration testing.

The idea for the Rocket Center, Space Camp, and the Saturn V exhibit came from Wernher von Braun. From the time he and his countrymen arrived in Huntsville in 1950, they embraced their rural Alabama home. They established a symphony orchestra, promoted a state university branch campus, and encouraged aerospace companies to locate regional offices there. Many, including von Braun, became American citizens. Despite their German accents and the bitter memories of World War II, these scientists created a legacy of friendship and respect. In

1975, Huntsville named its civic arts and convention center in honor of Wernher von Braun.

In a quiet corner of the Space Center's museum, little noticed by most visitors, is an old bicycle, the one Magnus von Braun rode down the mountain in Bavaria, never dreaming of the epochal ride into outer space and the extraordinary technology that would follow.

WEBSITES

U.S. Space & Rocket Center, www.rocketcenter.com

Marshall Space Flight Center, www.nasa.gov/centers/marshall/home/

Von Braun Center, www.vonbrauncenter.com

Space Camp, www.spacecamp.com

48

MAGIC KINGDOMS

ORLANDO, CELEBRATION, AND MAITLAND, FLORIDA

Maitland Art & History Museums

A few months before his death in 1966, Walt Disney announced plans to build EPCOT, the Experimental Prototype Community of Tomorrow, in central Florida. His dream was to adapt "the new ideas and new technologies that are now emerging from the creative centers of American industry . . . EPCOT will always be a showcase to the world for the ingenuity and imagination of American free enterprise . . . a planned, controlled community and a showcase for American industry and research, schools, cultural and educational opportunities." He envisioned a model city of 20,000 residents with "no retirees; everyone must be employed." With a commitment to continuous innovation, Disney envisioned a community that "will never be completed."

After Disney died, the Walt Disney Company lost interest in EPCOT, especially the idea of a planned residential community. The company was already fully engaged in building what it called "the Florida project," a theme park on 30,000 acres southwest of Orlando. In 1967, the Florida legislature gave the company nearly complete control over the entire parcel. Four years later, the Magic Kingdom opened as the first park in Walt Disney World Resort, now the world's most popular tourist destination.

Disney gave people what they expected. The character Mickey Mouse, for example, has appeared in every Disney medium from films and television to merchandise and theme parks. The designs of Disneyland in California and the Magic Kingdom at Disney World are almost identical, from the entrance down Main Street to Cinderella's castle to rides in Fantasyland, Frontierland, Tomorrowland, and Adventureland.

At the same time, Walt Disney was relentlessly committed to innovation, what he called the "plussing" factor. As a young filmmaker, he was the first to add dialogue and music in cartoons. He won Academy Awards for introducing Technicolor (1932) and for creating *Snow White and the Seven Dwarfs* (1937), the first feature-length animated film. To make *Fantasia* (1940), he created Fantasound, a sound reproduction system.

At Disneyland in California, he established Disney Imagineering, a team of engineers, designers, artists, architects, writers, and other specialists whose purpose was to "make the magic" that gave the park its distinctive character. The Imagineers designed Disneyland, Walt Disney World, and all the Disney theme parks as if they were making a movie, an integrated experience that felt like a performance rather than a series of disconnected rides. They used concepts such as "forced perspective," architectural illusions that made some buildings, like Cinderella's Castle and the Main Street buildings, look larger than they actually are. They invented Audio-Animatronics, robotic figures that moved and spoke, the first being the animatronic of Abraham Lincoln delivering the Gettysburg Address at the 1964 World's Fair in New York.

Disney conceived EPCOT as another opportunity to showcase the talents of his Imagineers. But without Disney, the Imagineers could not agree on whether EPCOT would be a display of cutting-edge technology or an exhibition of international cultures. When EPCOT opened in 1982 it offered both ideas with nine corporate-sponsored technology exhibitions and pavilions representing eleven nations, a never-ending world's fair.

In the 1990s the Walt Disney Company revived the idea of a planned residential community that would provide housing, transportation, health care, education, and recreation. They called it Celebration, located eight miles south of EPCOT, established as an unincorporated town in 1994. Unlike EPCOT, which promised a utopia through technology and continuous change, Celebration drew its inspiration from history and the timeless values of small-town America. Celebration reflected a growing trend in the 1990s known as New Urbanism that rejected suburban ideals characterized by dependency on the automobile and identical single-family homes dispersed on large lots. Instead, Celebration offered high-density pedestrian-friendly neighborhoods with diverse housing styles and ample public space.

Master planners Jaquelin T. Robertson and Robert A. M. Stern enlisted many of America's leading postmodern architects, such as Philip Johnson, Michael Graves, Charles Moore, and Cesar Pelli, to design Celebration's public buildings. Residential neighborhoods reflected period architecture, including Victorian, Colonial Revival, Spanish Mission, and Bungalow styles. The new approach to town planning, the diversity of housing styles, and especially the popularity of the Walt Disney Company drew thousands of people when the first housing lotteries were held in 1995. After nearly twenty years, the reaction to Celebration is divided; many residents and tourists praise the attractive architecture, the easy access to parks, and the small-town, neighborly environment. Critics describe the town as inauthentic, catering to a false and forced nostalgia. It is as if the town is an extension of the nearby theme parks. In one major respect, Celebration is like most American suburbs: its 2014 population of 7,500 is 90 percent white.

A third notable utopian vision in central Florida preceded both EPCOT and Celebration. In Maitland, about ten miles north of Orlando, Jules Andre Smith, an artist and architect, founded an artists' retreat in 1937 that flourished for twenty years under his personal supervision. This nearly six-acre complex consists of a Research Studio and the chapels, constructed from 1937 to 1942. The twenty-two concrete and stucco structures within this site represent America's best collection of Mayan and Aztec Revival art. Smith and his assistants decorated these buildings with more than two hundred concrete sculptures, carvings, murals, and reliefs—all produced on-site by hand—that reflect Mayan, Aztec, Christian, Asian, African, and mythological themes. The influence of Frank Lloyd Wright, who used Mayan themes in his early work, is evident in both the materials and the decorations at Maitland, with an astonishing assemblage of natural scenes, iconography, allegories, and fantasy characters that sprouted from Smith's very fertile imagination.

Smith's project benefited from the patronage of Mary Curtis Bok, whose father published the *Ladies' Home Journal*, and whose wealth helped start the Curtis Music Institute in Philadelphia. She saw the Maitland artists' retreat as a complement to the music program.

Bok's generosity supported fellowships for artists who lived and worked at the Research Studio each winter. Milton Avery, Jan Gelb, Teng Chiu, Ralston Crawford, and Consuelo Kanaga were some of the prominent artists who came to Maitland attracted by good weather and the opportunity to experiment with new forms and techniques. Smith's charismatic personality was also a major attraction. Even as his health declined in his later years, he was dreaming about new projects such as the Folklore Village he and anthropologist Zora Neale Hurston proposed for Eatonville, her hometown adjacent to Maitland.

After Smith's death in 1959, the Research Studio closed and his friends and other artists lobbied to preserve his art and buildings. In 1969, the city of Maitland purchased the site and later entrusted the daily operations to the Maitland Art & History Museums, a nonprofit organization that maintains the campus, designated a National Historic Landmark in 2014, and interprets Smith's creative achievements. A trip to Maitland, EPCOT, and Celebration provides a good introduction to the possibilities and limitations of creating community through art, technology, and central planning.

WEBSITES

EPCOT at Walt Disney World Resort, disneyworld.disney.go.com
    /destinations/epcot
Celebration, www.celebration.fl.us
Maitland Art & History Museums, www.artandhistory.org

NEARBY PLACES

Florida Southern College, www.flsouthern.edu
Zora Neale Hurston National Museum of Fine Arts,
    www.zoranealehurstonmuseum.com

49

SILICON VALLEY

PALO ALTO, CALIFORNIA

The Computer History Museum

"At different times in the past," Steve Jobs once said, "there were companies that exemplified Silicon Valley. It was Hewlett-Packard for a long time. Then, in the semiconductor era, it was Fairchild and Intel. . . . And then today, I think it's Apple and Google" (*Steve Jobs*, Walter Isaacson, 2011).

Jobs's brief history of the forty-mile corridor south of San Francisco synthesizes a technological revolution that transformed a region known for fruit orchards and food processing plants into a worldwide symbol of innovation. This change began in 1891 when railroad magnate Leland Stanford opened a university bearing his name in Palo Alto. One graduate was Frederick Terman, a chemistry and electrical engineering major, who joined the faculty in 1925. Over the next forty years, Terman was known as the unofficial founder of Silicon Valley, encouraging his students to start new technology companies near Stanford.

Two students, William Hewlett and David Packard, rented a Palo Alto garage—367 Addison Avenue—in 1938 and developed an audio oscillator, an improved low-cost version of an earlier device, that produced one pure tone at a time. Their first customer, Walt Disney Studios, bought eight oscillators to use in the production of the movie *Fantasia*. The following year the two men formed Hewlett-Packard, Inc., popularly known as HP. (A coin toss decided name order.) HP quickly outgrew the garage where it began, and embarked on a remarkable period of innovation, producing printers, cameras, scanners, calculators, data recorders, and computers.

HP and other electronics companies flourished during and after World War II through the burgeoning aviation, missile defense, and aerospace industries. In 1951, Frederick Terman promoted the establishment of Stanford Industrial Park (now the Stanford Research Park), a 660-acre facility that offered low-cost space and access to university research. Spurred by the Cold War with the Soviet Union, enormous federal contracts flowed into technology companies and university engineering programs centered in the South Bay of San Francisco, what we now call Silicon Valley.

The second person to shape the rise of Silicon Valley was William Shockley, one of the inventors in 1948 of the transistor, a device that could replace the bulky, fragile, and power-hungry vacuum-tube technology of that era. Shockley located his company in Mountain View near Stanford to manufacture semiconductors. He recruited talented engineers, but within a year conflicts with Shockley caused eight engineers to leave and form their own company, Fairchild Semiconductor.

Fairchild pioneered in the use of silicon, an inexpensive material, to make semiconductors. One of Fairchild's founders, Robert Noyce, developed the first commercially viable integrated circuit, or microchip, a technology breakthrough that revolutionized electronics. Used in everything from pocket calculators to spaceships, microchips made possible the low-cost production of TVs, radios, watches, stereos, and computers. The phenomenal growth of the semiconductor industry caused another Fairchild founder, Gordon Moore, to offer a theory in 1965 (updated in 1975) that the number of transistors in a microchip will double every two years. For the past fifty years, Moore's Law, as it has come to be known, has influenced the business decisions of many technology companies around the world. In 1968, Moore and Noyce founded Intel and hired Andrew Grove, a Hungarian-born engineer, as the first employee. In 1971, Intel produced the world's first commercially available microprocessor, a complete central processing unit on a single chip. The microprocessor reduced the cost of producing computers and set the stage for the personal computer revolution.

By 1970, journalists began using the name "Silicon Valley" in reference to the main element in microchips to describe the place where innovative companies such as HP and Intel flourished. By 1983, more than seven hundred electronics-related companies operated in the valley. One of those companies got its start in the mid-1970s when Steve Wozniak, an engineer at HP, began building a small, low-cost computer with his friend Steve Jobs. They presented a prototype to a group of hobbyists called the Homebrew Computer Club, then set up a workshop in Jobs's garage at 2066 Crist Drive in Los Altos, where they produced their first personal computer in 1976. A year later, they incorporated Apple, Inc., and in that same garage built the color Apple II, selling sixteen million computers in six years. In 1984, Apple produced a fully integrated computer, the Macintosh, that had a graphical user interface (developed by Xerox at its Palo Alto Research Center) in which a device called a "mouse" allowed a person to point to something on the computer screen, click on a word or image, and link to additional content. By 2010, Apple, Inc., propelled by its slogan "Think Different" and by Steve Jobs's singular gifts for product development, marketing, and design, had become the largest company in the world.

Another revolution, also with roots in Silicon Valley, took shape through the internet, created in 1974 by Vint Cerf and other faculty at Stanford. One of the applications of the internet was the World Wide Web, developed in 1989, which transformed commerce, education, and entertainment. One company, Google, ultimately dominated the internet, also called the Information Superhighway. Stanford University graduates Sergey Brin and Larry Page established the company in another garage, this one at 232 Santa Margarita Avenue in Menlo Park, in 1998. They created a search engine to quickly provide free access to information and entertainment. Google made money—more than $57 billion in gross revenue in 2013—by selling ads on its site and also by creating its own content and products. As Google and other technology companies continue to evolve, it is likely that mobile devices will overtake the personal computer as the primary source of communication and information.

Most of Silicon Valley's historic landmarks are corporate campuses closed to the public. However, several museums provide excellent introductions to the digital revolution. The best of these is the Computer History Museum in Mountain View, whose building is itself an artifact of high-tech history. It was built in 1994 by Silicon Graphics, Inc., a company founded in 1981 by Stanford graduates that faltered in the 1990s and declared bankruptcy in 2002.

While it is true that government support created the financial underpinnings for the digital revolution—from the first computer, ENIAC, to the creation of the internet—there remains a romantic fascination with solitary inventors working with meager resources like Edison, Ford, and the Wright brothers. The garage workshops of Silicon Valley—all located within fifteen miles of Palo Alto—have become tourist attractions, like the homes of Hollywood movie stars, symbols of individual innovation and a technological revolution that is still changing the world.

WEBSITES
Computer History Museum, www.computerhistory.org
Lemelson Center for the Study of Invention & Innovation,
    www.invention.si.edu
HP garage, www8.hp.com/us/en/hp-information/about-hp/history
    /hp-garage/hp-garage.html

NEARBY PLACES
The Tech Museum of Innovation, www.thetech.org
Intel Museum, www.intel.com/content/www/us/en/company-overview
    /intel-museum.html

50

MALLS OF AMERICA
EDINA AND BLOOMINGTON, MINNESOTA

Southdale Center

More than 75,000 people lined up to see Southdale, America's first enclosed shopping mall, when it opened in Edina, Minnesota, in 1956. The mall's designer, Victor Gruen, was an Austrian-born socialist who arrived in New York in 1938 with, as he recalled, "an architect's degree, eight dollars, and no English." Gruen integrated his professional training with experience in Viennese theater and a fervent belief in the social benefits of capitalism. He achieved success first as a store designer in New York, where he introduced "the Gruen transfer," which encouraged a pedestrian to leave a city sidewalk, enter a small recessed lobby surrounded by windows filled with merchandise, and become a consumer. He expanded his architectural practice to suburban sites, providing him with an opportunity to translate his concepts of community planning into reality. A well-designed shopping center, he argued, could overcome the failings of cities by providing a safe, attractive, and humane environment for customers and a profit center for merchants.

Gruen's first shopping center, Northland Center, opened outside Detroit in 1954, with new features such as a grocery, an auditorium, sculpture, and pedestrian walkways. That same year, Congress enacted legislation encouraging investment in manufacturing and commercial development, including a provision in the tax code for accelerated depreciation. Developers could now deduct their investments according to a schedule that significantly reduced, and often eliminated, their tax bill.

The passage of the Interstate Highway Act in 1956 led to rapid commercial growth in the suburbs. In Minneapolis, the Dayton Company, owners of a thriving downtown department store, commissioned Victor Gruen to design an enclosed climate-controlled shopping center in Edina, about ten miles south of the city. Southdale instantly became the standard for mall design. Gruen placed two large department stores, called "anchors," at each end of the mall, and connected them with two levels of smaller stores. To reach escalators located near the department stores, customers had to walk a continuous loop past the mall's seventy-two stores. But Gruen's mall was not just a collection of shops. He created a small town with a post office, a bank, a grocery store, birdcages, a petting zoo, a fountain, and a café. In the center was a town square he called the Garden Court of Springtime, a sunlit space for informal gathering and special events. Surrounding the mall were acres of free parking designed so that people could park on multiple levels and enter near their desired destination.

Southdale was popular, and people who grew up around Edina have warm memories of the mall's European village environment. It also earned praise from politicians and the media. However, Gruen's master plan for Southdale, a plan that included residences, offices, a lake, schools, and medical facilities, was never realized. Southdale's financial success inspired imitation—and competition—from malls in neighboring suburbs, and in response its owners expanded and drastically altered Gruen's original plan.

Southdale opened during one of the great migrations in American history as World War II veterans settled their families in suburbia, the vast spaces surrounding urban centers. They were following a tradition that began in the nineteenth century in response to the problems of cities—crime, corruption, and pollution. Writer Catherine E. Beecher encouraged this trend as coauthor (with her sister, Harriet Beecher Stowe) of *The American Woman's Home* (1869), a bestselling guide to managing a suburban home and garden. Passenger railroads and streetcars further contributed to suburban growth, and developers commissioned urban planners and landscape architects like John Nolen, Earle Draper, and the Olmsted brothers to design residential subdivisions. Sears, Roebuck sold mail-order house kits—over fifty thousand between 1908 and 1940—to do-it-yourself builders.

Following World War II the suburbs grew exponentially. Owning a home represented the fulfillment of the American Dream, an ideal articulated by James Truslow Adams in 1931. He maintained that life in America "should be better and richer and fuller . . . with opportunity for each." This powerful concept drove the rise of suburbia along with low-interest veterans' loans, tax deductions for mortgage interest, and the growth in automobile ownership. The percentage of Americans living in suburbs rose from 23 in 1950 to 37 in 1970 to 50 in 2000.

Not everyone admired the impact of suburbia. Civil rights leaders noted that many new suburban communities excluded African Americans. Social critics like David Riesman (*The Lonely Crowd*, 1950) and William Whyte (*The Organization Man*, 1956) described the conformity and consumerism of postwar society, and Betty Friedan (*The Feminine Mystique*, 1963) challenged the traditional role of women as contented domestic managers. Even Victor Gruen became disillusioned by suburban sprawl and returned to Austria in 1968.

Nevertheless, America's malls kept growing. In 1992, the Mall of America (MOA) opened in Bloomington, Minnesota, a few miles from Southdale. With 520 stores, 5,000,000 square feet, and parking for 12,000 cars, it dwarfed anything previously built in this country. Dubbed "Hugedale" and "Sprawl of America" by critics, MOA attempted to incorporate Victor Gruen's philosophy by offering an indoor amusement park, an aquarium, and a full schedule of performances. However, because of its enormous size and large crowds, it could not replicate the intimate, communal feeling of Southdale and other centers.

By 2000, the financial vitality of shopping malls was eroding. Discount department stores like Walmart dominated the retail industry. The convenience of online shopping made companies like Amazon serious competitors to traditional retail centers. The Great Recession of 2008 hit retail shopping malls especially hard. Some companies adapted to this new environment. The Dayton Company, founder of Southdale, started its own discount store, Target, in 1962 and over the next fifty years introduced online shopping, pop-up stores, and urban shopping centers. Nevertheless, many American shopping malls, including Brookdale just outside Minneapolis, were closing. Of the one thousand shopping malls in the United States in 2014, about half were projected to shut down within twenty years.

Contrary to this trend, the Mall of America continues to flourish. In 2004, the city of Minneapolis built a light rail connection linking MOA and downtown. In 2014, the mall's owners, subsidized by tax incentives, announced a $325 million expansion with new stores, a hotel, offices, event space, and a goal to increase the number of visitors, already at forty million annually, by 50 percent. MOA's announcement confirmed that suburban shopping malls have become entertainment centers and tourist attractions, hardly the self-contained commercial villages envisioned by Victor Gruen in the 1950s.

WEBSITES
Southdale Center, www.simon.com/mall/southdale-center
Mall of America, www.mallofamerica.com

NEARBY PLACES
Minnesota History Center, www.minnesotahistorycenter.org
Mill City Museum, www.millcitymuseum.org

ACKNOWLEDGMENTS

The idea for *50 Great American Places* grew out of a conversation with David McCullough. Our friendship began in the 1980s when we discovered our mutual interest in historic preservation and historical literacy, and I have had the privilege of joining David and his wife, Rosalee, on many occasions to promote that cause. I am especially grateful to him for writing the foreword and for introducing me to Bob Bender at Simon & Schuster, whose editorial judgment has been enormously valuable. Bob and his assistant, Johanna Li, have guided me through the publication process with patience and good humor. I am indebted to Judy Steer for her excellent copyediting.

As I visited the essential historic sites across the United States, I was fortunate to meet people who generously shared their knowledge and very willingly provided photographs and editorial suggestions. Their passion for their respective historic sites and the stories they represent reminded me of what a privilege it is to be a member of the public history community. I wish to thank Leith Adams, Deborah Barnhardt, Kimberly Bender, Eric Blind, Carol Bodas, Leslie Bowman, Kimberly Brengle, Danny Brucker, Charles Bryan, Amanda Bryden, Burl Burlingam, Brian Cannon, Kirk Christensen, Thomas Colligan, Andrea Cox, Leonard DeGraef, Tony Doughty, Richard Dressner, Brett Egan, Russ Fabre, Jan

Gallimore, Judy Geniac, Noemi Ghazala, Jodi Glass, Steve Gragert, Barbara Hall, Katherine Hamilton-Smith, Stanley Hirsch, John Hollar, Bill Iseminger, Carol Johnson, Dan Jordan, Michael Kaiser, Katherine Kane, Cynthia Kelly, Patrick Ladden, Joanne Lee, Fran Levine, Tia Lombardi, David Margolick, Gwen Mayer, Tom Mellins, Craig Middelton, Patricia Mooradian, Mark Oland, Ashley Olson, Christian Overland, Johanna Pedersen, Mimi Quintanilla, Anne Rashford, David Reynolds, Thom Rosenblum, Eric Seiferth, Dick Sellars, Dedie Snow, Dag Spicer, John Stoudt, Kimberly Szewczyk, Michael Taylor, Carolyn Tinker, Shauna Tonkin, Ann Toplovich, Lori Urso, Mark Varien, John Vidal, Connie Weinzapfel, Donna Williams, Courtney Wilson, and Bill Withuhn.

I benefited from support from several people whose skills were important in moving my research forward. Thanks to an appointment as a senior scholar at the Woodrow Wilson International Center for Scholars in Washington, D.C., I was able to work with a resourceful intern, Cara Whiting, who provided bibliographical research. During the final stages of writing, the Amagansett Free Public Library in Amagansett, New York, proved to be an excellent place for research and editing. Three administrative assistants worked with me at various times in my office at the Heurich House Museum—Hilary Strimple, who managed schedules and organizational issues; Courtney Hobson, who researched websites and photo archives; and Hannah Saloio, who selected the final list of photo images and secured permissions. Thanks to David Sonenberg and Bill Schecter for their friendship and good advice, and to Tony Kornheiser and Keith Glass for tips on how to become a successful author.

My family played an important part in creating this book. My son, Loren, joined me on many field trips to museums and historic sites. I am especially grateful to my wife, Cathryn Keller, who made the journey to more sites than I can count, and who read and critiqued nearly every essay in this book. Her insights into the importance of the American West shaped my research and the selection of several sites. Without her encouragement, I am not sure I would have finished the task.

BIBLIOGRAPHY

There are several excellent overviews of American history that offer a context for historic places.

Cullen, Jim. *The American Dream.* New York: Oxford University Press, 2003.

Foner, Eric. *The Story of American Freedom.* New York: W. W. Norton & Company, 1998.

Foner, Eric, and John A. Garrity, eds. *The Reader's Companion to American History.* Boston: Houghton Mifflin, 1991.

Graham, Wade. *American Eden.* New York: Harper, 2011.

Johnson, Paul. *A History of the American People.* New York: HarperCollins, 1997.

Kammen, Michael. *Mystic Chords of Memory.* New York: Vintage Books, 1991.

The National Parks: Shaping the System. Washington, D.C.: National Park Service, 1991.

Sources for specific historic sites include the following books and articles:

1. THE NATIONAL MALL

Gopnik, Adam. "Stones and Bones: Visiting the 9/11 Memorial and Museum." *The New Yorker* (July 7 and 14, 2014): 38–44.

Lewis, Michael J. "The Decline of American Monuments and Memorials," *Imprimis* 41, no. 4 (April 2012).

Penczer, Peter R. *The Washington National Mall.* Arlington, Virginia: Oneonta Press, 2007.

2. THE MOUNDS AND THE ARCH

Iseminger, William. *Cahokia Mounds: America's First City.* Charleston, S.C.: History Press, 2010.

Lewis, Wallace G. *In the Footsteps of Lewis and Clark: Early Commemorations and the Origins of the National Historic Trail.* Boulder: University Press of Colorado, 2010.

Pauketat, Timothy. *Cahokia.* New York: Penguin Books, 2009.

Sandweiss, Eric. *St. Louis: The Evolution of an American Urban Landscape.* Philadelphia: Temple University Press, 2001.

3. MESA VERDE

Houk, Rose. *Cliff Palace.* Mesa Verde National Park: Mesa Verde Museum Association, 2011.

Kohler, Timothy A., Mark Varien, and Aaron Wright, eds. *Leaving Mesa Verde: Peril and Change in the Thirteenth-Century Southwest.* Tucson: University of Arizona Press, 2010.

4. THE PALACE OF THE GOVERNORS

Abbink, Emily. *New Mexico's Palace of the Governors: History of an American Treasure.* Santa Fe: Museum of New Mexico Press, 2007.

Kelly, James, and Barbara Clark Smith. *Jamestown, Québec, Santa Fe: Three North American Beginnings.* Washington, D.C.: Smithsonian Books, 2007.

Wilson, Chris. *The Myth of Santa Fe.* Albuquerque: University of New Mexico Press, 1997.

5. WITCH TRIALS

Rosenthal, Bernard. *Salem Story: Reading the Witch Trials of 1692.* Cambridge, U.K.: Cambridge University Press, 1993.

Vowell, Sarah. *The Wordy Shipmates.* New York: Riverhead Books, 2008.

6. BOUNDARY LINE

Danson, Edwin. *Drawing the Line: How Mason and Dixon Surveyed the Most Famous Border in America.* New York: Wiley, 2000.

Shorto, Russell. *The Island at the Center of the World: The Epic Story of Dutch Manhattan and the Forgotten Colony That Shaped America.* New York: Vintage Books, 2004.

Stein, Mark. *How the States Got Their Shapes.* New York: Smithsonian, 2008.

7. FORKS OF THE OHIO

Chernow, Ron. *Washington: A Life.* New York: Penguin, 2011.

Miller, Randall, and William Pencak, eds. *Pennsylvania, A History of the Commonwealth.* University Park: Pennsylvania State University Press, 2002.

8. FREEDOM TRAIL

Bahne, Charles. *The Complete Guide to Boston's Freedom Trail.* Cambridge, Mass.: Newtowne, 2005.

McCullough, David. *1776.* New York: Simon & Schuster, 2005.

———. *John Adams.* New York: Simon & Schuster, 2001.

Whitehill, Walter Muir, and Lawrence W. Kennedy. *Boston: A Topographical History.* Cambridge, Mass.: Belknap Press, 2000.

9. THE LIBERTY BELL

Isaacson, Walter. *Benjamin Franklin.* New York: Simon & Schuster, 2003.

Nash, Gary B. *The Liberty Bell.* New Haven: Yale University Press, 2010.

10. VIRGINIA PENINSULA

Isaac, Rhys. *The Transformation of Virginia, 1740–1790*. Chapel Hill: University of North Carolina Press, 1982.

Rubel, David. *America's War of Independence, 1763–1783: A Concise Illustrated History of the American Revolution*. New York: Silver Moon Press, 1992.

11. MONTICELLO

Andrews, Wayne. *Pride of the South: A Social History of Southern Architecture*. New York: Atheneum, 1979.

Gordon-Reed, Annette. *The Hemingses of Monticello: An American Family*. New York: W. W. Norton & Company, 2008.

Jefferson, Thomas. *The Life and Morals of Jesus of Nazareth*. Washington, D.C.: Smithsonian Books, 2011.

12. THE PRESIDIO AT THE GOLDEN GATE

Brook, James, Chris Carlsson, and Nancy Peters, eds. *Reclaiming San Francisco: History, Politics, Culture*. San Francisco: City Lights Books, 1998.

Halloran, Pete. "Seeing the Trees Through the Forest: Oaks and History in the Presidio." In *Reclaiming San Francisco: History, Politics, Culture*. San Francisco: City Lights, 1998.

Kennedy, Roger. *Presidio Gateways: Views of a National Landmark at San Francisco's Golden Gate*. San Francisco: Chronicle Books, 1994.

Starr, Kevin. *Golden Gate: The Life and Times of America's Greatest Bridge*. New York: Bloomsbury Press, 2010.

13. WHITE DOVE OF THE DESERT

Sheridan, Thomas E. *Arizona: A History*. Tucson: University of Arizona Press, 1995.

14. SLATER MILL

Rivard, Paul E. *Samuel Slater: Father of American Manufacturers*. Pawtucket, R.I.: Slater Mill Historic Site, 1974.

15. VILLAGE GREEN

Reynolds, David S. *John Brown, Abolitionist: The Man Who Killed Slavery, Sparked the Civil War, and Seeded Civil Rights.* New York: Knopf, 2005.

16. TWO UTOPIAS

Bryden, Amanda S., and Connie A. Weinzapfel. "New Harmony at 200." *Traces of Indiana and Midwestern History* 26, no. 2 (spring 2014).

Carmony, Donald F., and Josephine Elliott. "New Harmony, Indiana." *Indiana Magazine of History* LXXVI (September 1980): 161–261.

Donnachie, Ian. *Robert Owen: Owen of New Lanark and New Harmony.* East Lothian, Scotland: Tuckwell Press, 2000.

Wilson, William E. *The Angel and the Serpent: The Story of New Harmony.* Bloomington: Indiana University Press, 1964.

17. RAILROAD UNIVERSITY OF THE UNITED STATES

Douglas, George H. *All Aboard: The Railroad in American Life.* New York: Smithmark, 1996.

Withuhn, William L. *Rails Across America: A History of Railroads in North America.* New York: Smithmark, 1993.

18. THE ALAMO

Flores, Richard R. *Remembering the Alamo: Memory, Modernity, and the Master Symbol.* Austin: University of Texas Press, 2002.

Hoyt, Edwin P. *The Alamo: An Illustrated History.* Lanham, Md.: Taylor Trade Publishing, 1999.

19. DECLARATION OF SENTIMENTS

Wellman, Judith. *The Road to Seneca Falls: Elizabeth Cady Stanton and the First Women's Rights Convention.* Urbana: University of Illinois Press, 2004.

20. TEMPLE SQUARE

Beam, Alex. *American Crucifixion: The Murder of Joseph Smith and the Fate of the Mormon Church.* New York: Public Affairs, 2014.

Gopnik, Adam. "I, Nephi." *The New Yorker* (August 13 & 20, 2012): 78–86.

Reynolds, David S. *Waking Giant: America in the Age of Jackson.* New York: Harper, 2008.

21. FORT SUMTER

McPherson, James M. *Battle Cry of Freedom: The Civil War Era.* New York: Oxford University Press, 1988.

Roland, Charles P. *An American Iliad: The Story of the Civil War.* New York: McGraw-Hill, 1991.

Rosen, Robert N. *A Short History of Charleston.* San Francisco: Lexikos, 1982.

22. NEW BIRTH OF FREEDOM

Faust, Drew Gilpin. *This Republic of Suffering: Death and the American Civil War.* New York: Knopf, 2008.

Ward, Geoffrey. *The Civil War: An Illustrated History.* New York: Knopf, 1990.

23. SCHOOLHOUSE AND FIELDHOUSE

Geiger, Roger L., and Nathan M. Sorber. *The Land-Grant Colleges and the Reshaping of American Higher Education.* Piscataway, N.J.: Transaction Publishers, 2013.

Patterson, James T. *Brown v. Board of Education: A Civil Rights Milestone and Its Troubled Legacy.* New York: Oxford University Press, 2001.

Pomerantz, Gary M. *Wilt, 1962: The Night of 100 Points and the Dawn of a New Era.* New York: Three Rivers Press, 2005.

24. FIRST NATIONAL PARK

Goodwin, Doris Kearns. *The Bully Pulpit: Theodore Roosevelt, William Howard Taft, and the Golden Age of Journalism.* New York: Simon & Schuster, 2013.

Muir, John. *Our National Parks.* Madison, Wis.: University of Wisconsin Press, 1981.

Schullery, Paul, and Lee Whittlesey. *Myth and History in the Creation of Yellowstone National Park.* Lincoln: University of Nebraska Press, 2003.

25. NOOK FARM NEIGHBORS: STOWE AND TWAIN

Kane, Katherine. "The Most Famous American in the World." *Connecticut Explored* 9, no. 3 (summer 2011): 20–25.

Kaplan, Justin. *Mr. Clemens and Mark Twain.* New York: Simon & Schuster, 1966.

Normen, Elizabeth J. "Where Mr. Twain and Mrs. Stowe Built Their Dream Houses." *Connecticut Explored* 9, no. 3 (summer 2011): 26–29.

26. WILLA CATHER'S GREAT PRAIRIE

Acocella, Joan. *Willa Cather and the Politics of Criticism.* New York: Vintage, 2000.

Lee, Hermione. *Willa Cather: Double Lives.* New York: Vintage Books, 1989.

27. INDIAN WARS

Brown, Dee. *Bury My Heart at Wounded Knee.* New York: Henry Holt and Company, 1970.

Caputo, Philip. *The Longest Road.* New York: Henry Holt and Company, 2013.

Ostler, Jeffrey. *The Plains Sioux and U.S. Colonialism from Lewis and Clark to Wounded Knee.* Cambridge, Mass.: Cambridge University Press, 2004.

Utley, Robert M. *The Lance and the Shield: The Life and Times of Sitting Bull.* New York: Henry Holt and Company, 1993.

Wilson, James. *The Earth Shall Weep: The History of Native America.* New York: Grove Press, 1998.

28. THE BRIDGE AND THE STATUE

Berenson, Edward. *The Statue of Liberty: A Transatlantic Story.* New Haven: Yale University Press, 2012.

Lopate, Phillip. *Waterfront: A Walk Around Manhattan.* New York: Anchor Books, 2004.

McCullough, David. *The Great Bridge: The Epic Story of the Building of the Brooklyn Bridge.* New York: Simon & Schuster, 1972.

29. EDISON'S LABORATORY

Stross, Randall E. *The Wizard of Menlo Park: How Thomas Alva Edison Invented the Modern World.* New York: Three Rivers Press, 2007.

30. WORLD'S COLUMBIAN EXPOSITION

Appelbaum, Stanley. *The Chicago World's Fair of 1893: A Photographic Record.* New York: Dover Publications, 1980.

Larson, Erik. *The Devil in the White City: Murder, Magic, and Madness at the Fair That Changed America.* New York: Vintage Books, 2003.

31. BILTMORE HOUSE

The Biltmore Company. *Biltmore: An American Masterpiece.* Asheville, N.C.: The Biltmore Company, 2012.

32. TALIESIN

Huxtable, Ada Louise. *Frank Lloyd Wright: A Life.* New York: Viking Penguin, 2004.

Wright, Frank Lloyd. *Frank Lloyd Wright: Writings and Buildings.* Edited by Edgar Kaufmann and Ben Raeburn. New York: Meridian, 1960.

33. FIRST FLIGHT

McCullough, David. *The Wright Brothers.* New York: Simon & Schuster, 2015.

Parramore, Thomas. *First to Fly: North Carolina and the Beginnings of Aviation.* Chapel Hill: University of North Carolina Press, 2002.

34. GRAND CENTRAL TERMINAL

Miller, Donald L. *Supreme City: How Jazz Age Manhattan Gave Birth to Modern America.* New York: Simon & Schuster, 2014.

Roberts, Sam. *Grand Central: How a Train Station Transformed America.* New York: Grand Central Publishing, 2013.

Stiles, T. J. *The First Tycoon: The Epic Life of Cornelius Vanderbilt.* New York: Knopf, 2009.

35. BIRTHPLACE OF JAZZ

Brothers, Thomas. *Louis Armstrong's New Orleans.* New York: W. W. Norton & Company, 2006.

Campanella, Richard. *Bienville's Dilemma: A Historical Geography of New Orleans.* Lafayette: University of Louisiana Press, 2008.

36. LEGENDARY HOLLYWOOD: WARNER BROS. STUDIO

Gabler, Neal. *An Empire of Their Own: How Jews Invented Hollywood.* New York: Crown, 1988.

Stein, Jean. "West of Eden." *The New Yorker* (February 16, 1998): 151–70.

"Warner Brothers." *Fortune* 16, no. 6 (December 1937): 109–13, 206–20.

37. FORD ROUGE

Cabadas, Joseph P. *River Rouge: Ford's Industrial Colossus.* St. Paul, Minn: Motorbooks, 2004.

38. WILL ROGERS HIGHWAY

Dedek, Peter. *Hip to the Trip: A Cultural History of Route 66.* Albuquerque: University of New Mexico Press, 2007.

Yagoda, Ben. *Will Rogers: A Biography.* New York: Knopf, 1993.

39. THE MOTHER CHURCH OF COUNTRY MUSIC

Carr, Patrick, ed. *The Illustrated History of Country Music.* New York: Random House, 1995.

Eiland, William U. *Nashville's Mother Church: The History of the Ryman Auditorium.* Nashville: Opryland USA, 1992.

Hagan, Chet. *Grand Ole Opry.* New York: Henry Holt and Company, 1989.

40. HOOVER DAM

Hiltzik, Michael. *Colossus: Hoover Dam and the Making of the American Century.* New York: Free Press, 2010.

Ketcham, Christopher. "Razing Arizona: Will Drought Destroy the Southwest?" *Harper's* 328, no. 1967 (April 2014): 53–64.

Reisner, Marc. *Cadillac Desert: The American West and Its Disappearing Water.* New York: Penguin Books, 1986.

41. PEARL HARBOR

Daws, Gavan. *Shoal of Time: A History of the Hawaiian Islands.* Honolulu: University of Hawaii Press, 1968.

Rosenberg, Emily S. *A Date Which Will Live: Pearl Harbor in American Memory.* Durham, N.C.: Duke University Press, 2003.

42. MINIDOKA CAMP

Hayashi, Brian Masarv. *Democratizing the Enemy: The Japanese American Internment.* Princeton, N.J.: Princeton University, 2004.

Tremayne, Russell, Todd Shallat, and Melissa Lavitt. *Surviving Minidoka: The Legacy of WWII Japanese American Incarceration.* Boise, Idaho: Boise State University, 2013.

43. MANHATTAN PROJECT

Kelly, Cynthia, ed. *The Manhattan Project: The Birth of the Atomic Bomb in the Words of Its Creators, Eyewitnesses, and Historians.* New York: Black Dog & Leventhal Publishers, 2007.

44. SWEET AUBURN

Jackson, Troy. *Becoming King: Martin Luther King Jr. and the Making of a National Leader.* Lexington: University Press of Kentucky, 2008.

45. CENTRAL HIGH SCHOOL

Beals, Melba Pattillo. *Warriors Don't Cry: A Searing Memoir of the Battle to Integrate Little Rock's Central High.* New York: Washington Square Press, 1994.

Deutsch, Stephanie. *You Need a Schoolhouse: Booker T. Washington, Julius Rosenwald, and the Building of Schools for the Segregated South.* Evanston, Illinois: Northwestern University Press, 2011.

Margolick, David. *Elizabeth and Hazel: Two Women of Little Rock.* New Haven: Yale University Press, 2011.

46. SALK INSTITUTE

Brownlee, David Bruce, and David Gilson De Long. *Louis I. Kahn: In the Realm of Architecture.* New York: Universe Publishing, 1997.

Jacobs, Charlotte De Gross. *Jonas Salk: A Life.* Oxford: Oxford University Press, 2015.

47. SATURN V ROCKET

Ward, Bob. *Dr. Space: The Life of Wernher von Braun.* Annapolis, Md.: Naval Institute Press, 2005.

48. MAGIC KINGDOMS

Hayden, Dolores. *Building Suburbia: Green Fields and Urban Growth, 1820–2000.* New York: Pantheon, 2003.

Thomas, Bob. *Walt Disney: An American Original.* New York: Disney
  Editions, 1976.

49. SILICON VALLEY

Auletta, Ken. *Googled: The End of the World as We Know It.* New York:
  Penguin Press, 2009.

Isaacson, Walter. *Steve Jobs.* New York: Simon & Schuster, 2011.

50. MALLS OF AMERICA

"Birth, Death and Shopping: The Rise and Fall of the Shopping Mall."
  The Economist, December 19, 2007.

Hardwick, M. Jeffrey. *Mall Maker: Victor Gruen, Architect of an American
  Dream.* Philadelphia: University of Pennsylvania Press, 2004.

INDEX

Page numbers in *italics* refer to illustrations.